MAKING SPEECH
(FOR YOU AND THE AUDIENCE)
How to Make a Pretty Good Speech Even Better!

BY MARK G. WOODS, PH.D
ILLUSTRATIONS BY JORDANA BITNER

Copyright ©2010 by Mark G. Woods, Ph.D. All rights reserved. Printed in the United States of America. No part of this book may be used or reproduced in any manner whatsoever without written permission from the author.

ISBN: 978-0-615-41576-5

CONTENTS

Introduction xiii

CHAPTER 1
RULES OF ENGAGEMENT (BEFORE YOU START A SPEECH)

You Love Public Speaking, You Just Don't Know It... Yet. 1

Four Simple Rules of Public Speaking 3

How to Quickly Improve as a Speaker 5

What Makes a Good Speech 'Good?' 6

How Long Should a Speech Be? 9

Just One Thing 12

CHAPTER 2
AUDIENCES AND TOPICS

The Audience: What It's All About 14

Know Your Audience 15

What's the Point? 17

Choosing a Topic 19

Provide Relevance to the Topic 22

Create the Audience to Create the Message. 24

Inspire the Audience. 26

Lives Are at Stake: Framing the Importance of the Message 28

Questions to Ask, Comments to Keep 30

CHAPTER 3
BUILDING THE SPEECH

The Importance of the Introduction 34

Crafting an Introduction 36

Jazz Up the Preview. 40

Building the Body (of the Speech) 42

In Conclusion, Say Something More 47

The Take-Away 50

Question as Transition?. 51

Edit for Effectiveness. 52

CHAPTER 4
TYPES OF SPEECHES

Informative Speeches—Teaching to the Choir. 55

Informative Speech Template. 57

Persuasive Speeches: Assessing the Need for Change 65

Persuasive Speech Template 69

Commemorative Speeches: Never Say 'Always' 78

Commemorative Speech Template. 81

After Dinner Speech: No Laughter Required. 84

Two-Point Business Presentation 88

Two-Point Business Presentation Template 91

Impromptu Speech 94

CHAPTER 5
RESEARCH—KNOW YOUR STUFF

Gathering Good Information. 98

Research Shows... 101

Expert Opinions Are Still Just Opinions 102

How to Cite Sources in a Speech. 104

Why Cite Sources in a Speech. 106

CHAPTER 6
DELIVERING THE SPEECH

Deliver More Impact. 109

The Solution for Eye Contact 112

Methods of Delivery—The Manuscript. 114

Methods of Delivery—Speaking from Memory 117

Methods of Delivery—Winging It (Impromptu Style). 118

Methods of Delivery—Using Brief Notes 120

Overcoming Your Fear 122

Don't Hide Behind Visual Aids. 125

Handle the Handouts 128

CHAPTER 7
PUBLIC SPEAKING AND BEYOND

Wanting and Working to Be a Great Speaker 130

Expand Beyond the Basics 132

Applying Skills Beyond the Obvious 135

Make It Better 137

Make It Better, Make It Shorter 138

What More Can I Say? 139

APPENDIX

Interviews: Applying Public Speaking Skills 141

For Students: The Secret to Success (in School) 144

INTRODUCTION

Do you break out in a cold sweat when someone asks you to speak to a group of people? The fear of public speaking is very normal. We spend most of our time *not* speaking to groups of people, so when we have to give a speech, we are often painfully aware of how little experience we have. It's very difficult to look good at anything when you've only done it a few times. It's that inexperience that makes you look or feel foolish, and no one likes that.

And, that's what this book (and my website www.prettygoodspeech.com) is all about. No one said you have to give a perfect speech. Wouldn't it be okay to do a pretty good job of things? It's not like you're a speaking professional. We're talking just one speech or one presentation. You just have to get through it, preferably without looking stupid.

This is where this book comes in.

IS IT REALLY THAT SIMPLE?

Getting up in public and speaking is not easy. Actually, it is easy, but we make it difficult. How do we make it difficult? Well, by…

- setting up excessively high expectations
- not understanding the fundamentals
- lack of experience

The problem is we want to be great speakers without preparing and having rarely done it. How many things can you do well the first time you tried it? My guess is: very few.

TRY THE PRETTY GOOD SPEECH... THEN MAKE IT EVEN BETTER!

We're not trying to turn you into a world-class public speaker or a world-class research analyst. We just want to give you the basics so that you can do a pretty good job of it.

Why? Well, ultimately, we believe that if you feel more confident about public speaking, you will be more inclined to do it. Communication skills are critical for future success (Don't believe us? Try going to a job interview, say nothing, and see if you get the job!), so it is extremely important for you to develop this skill set. With a little confidence that comes from knowing the basics and a little practice, your pretty good speeches might just lead to pretty great opportunities.

THE SECRET TO SUCCESSFUL SPEAKING

It's no secret; the only way to get good at something is to learn about it and to practice doing it. Along the way, you'll have good days and bad days. But, by understanding the basics of writing a speech, you'll feel a lot more comfortable giving the speech. That confidence boost will super charge your good days, and pull you through those bad days.

I've been teaching the skills of public speaking now for the past 10 years, and I tell everyone that it is possible to prepare a pretty good speech (as long as you actually want to). So far, I have not been disappointed.

It's really simple once you have the basics in place, and it gets better with time and effort.

So, this book will help provide you the encouragement you need. Along the way, I'll provide some tips that you can apply that hopefully will have an immediate and positive impact for you. Some advice will apply to students, some will apply to working professionals, and most of it should be universal.

Let's get started!

CHAPTER 1

RULES OF ENGAGEMENT
(Before You Start a Speech)

YOU LOVE PUBLIC SPEAKING, YOU JUST DON'T KNOW IT... YET

What's really going on when you get up there to speak? A feeling of dread fills you and you are certain you will not survive the experience. You start to sweat; your knees feel weak, and throwing up seems like a pretty good idea, or do I exaggerate?

Believe it or not, you love that feeling. You just don't realize it. But you will.

The Roller-Coaster Ride

What happens when you go to your favorite amusement park? You stand in line for hours waiting to get on the roller-coaster. It's not exciting, but you endure it because when you finally get on the roller-coaster... what a rush!

So, as you begin to climb up into the air, you hear a weird sound: tink, tink, tink. Guess what? That's the seconds of your life ticking away, and you don't even realize it. Actually, you do, and you begin to feel something in the pit of your stomach. Call it butterflies or nerves; it is adrenalin pumping through your body. You are reacting to the stress. You look at your friend sitting next to you and you say excitedly, "This is so awesome!" And it is.

You zoom down and back up and all around at dizzying speeds. Incredibly, you survive. And with flushed expressions of excitement, you say to your friend, "Let's do it again!" And you do.

Roller-Coaster Speech

Now, it's your turn to get up to speak. You stand up and you start to walk to the podium. Oddly, you hear a sound: tink, tink, tink. It's the seconds of your life ticking away, only this time you *know* you're going to die. You start to feel that feeling in the pit of your stomach. Call it butterflies or nerves; it is adrenalin pumping through your body. You are reacting to the stress. You look at your co-workers or classmates and say to yourself, "this is not so awesome." Actually, you probably say, "I'm sick. I'm going to throw up. I hate this. I don't want to die!"

And you don't, but when it's over you say, "I never want to do that again."

Good versus Bad Adrenalin?

You had two very different experiences, or did you? You had a moment of stress and your body produced adrenalin. That's about the same. The only difference was in how you reacted to that stress. At the amusement park, you enjoyed the feeling of adrenalin running through you. At the speaker's podium, you felt nausea from the adrenalin running through you. What was the difference?

It's not good adrenalin and bad adrenalin. It's just adrenalin. The difference is what you decided the experience to be. When you are placed in a situation, you decide whether or not you enjoy it. If you decide that roller-coaster rides are tons of fun, then they are. And, if you decide that public speaking is a painful experience, then it is.

So, could you decide that public speaking might just be the ultimate adrenalin rush? Could it be something you enjoy just because you decided it was enjoyable?

You can say "no" if you want to. You can also say, "Yes." The experience is yours, so the choice is yours. What do you want it to be?

FOUR SIMPLE RULES OF PUBLIC SPEAKING

You stand up, you start to feel your body heat rising, you lower your head, and you say in the dullest voice possible, "This speech is on butterflies..." The crowd inwardly groans. You feel their pain, but your only concern is getting the speech done and over. You power through it, say "that's it," and walk back to a smattering of half-hearted applause. You realize that your speech was not of any value, but you think, "I don't care. At least I'm done." You know you can do better, but you chose not to. Why take the chance of looking and feeling any dumber up there? I paint a grim picture, but I don't think I exaggerate.

How did it get this way? More importantly, what can we do?

It started somewhere in high school... maybe middle school. You somehow became self-aware. This usually happens when you recognize someone is more talented than you along some line. For example, I remember singing at the top of my lungs when I was in third grade. We all did. We all loved it. But, one day, I realized that my voice sounded different than others. I think it was in eighth grade and the choir teacher made me sing alone. She told me to move up to the bass section. I realized that I was different, as I'm sure others discovered. We then make a judgment as to whether the difference is good or bad, better or worse. If it's bad or worse, we move away from it. And, yes, I stopped choir once I got into high school and took art!

As soon as we note the differences, we try to minimize our exposed weaknesses. Almost universally, this seems to be public speaking. So, we speak as quickly as we can. Not only that, but we try to hide our weaknesses by being purposefully bad. This way, when someone says, "That sucked," you can say, "Of course it did. I did it on purpose."

And what, exactly, do we do? Well, we write poorly, speak softly and in a monotone reading voice, and avert eye contact. We do everything incorrectly, and so does everyone else— no deviation from the norm.

But, here's the problem: if you don't stand out from the crowd, then you don't get noticed by those who can make a difference.

If you practice doing poorly, then you will perform poorly. You'll get used to it and come to expect that you are doing it the way it is supposed to be done. And, maybe it's no worse than anyone else, but you aren't going to do yourself any favors. Think about that: if you are interviewing for a job or a raise, and all things being equal (qualifications), what will they judge you by? The answer: how well you present yourself at the interview.

Try mumbling in a monotone voice poorly crafted sentences while avoiding eye contact and see if you get the job.

Or, you can follow some simple rules and improve by leaps and bounds.

Rule #1
Never start a speech by saying, "This speech is about..."

It's as if you are saying, "This speech is so bad, I need to tell you right away what the topic is, otherwise, you wouldn't know." Instead, try asking a rhetorical question that will pique the audience's interest or provide some statistic that will lead into your topic.

Rule #2
Never end a speech by saying "That's it."

Again, it's like saying, "This speech is so bad, you wouldn't even know it was finished unless I told you it was over." I realize that it's difficult, but this is where you get a golden opportunity to address the audience more personally. Since you are in the conclusion, summarize the main ideas of the speech, and urge them toward some action (if it's a persuasive speech) or give them the next step (if it's an informative speech). Encourage them. Assure them. Give them some hope. Then, instead of saying "that's it," say, "Thank you."

Rule #3
Put some emotion into the speech.

I'm not asking you to scream and shout or weep or laugh hysterically. Just add a little care into your voice. Stress words that are important. Speak to the audience as if they were your closest friend in need of your advice. It's something you do all the time, so you don't need lessons in technique. All you need to do is care, and allow others to hear it in your voice.

Rule #4
Look them in their eyes.

You also show you care by actually looking into their eyes. I realize it's a daunting task, but the audience needs to see that you are talking *to* them and not *at* them. Looking into their eyes allows that connection, which allows them to know you really do care.

It's funny, but some of my favorite singers aren't always the best singers vocally. But, they have an honesty and depth of feeling that comes through in their voice that is so compelling. So, it's not about how technically proficient someone is as a speaker; it's a matter of heart. And, that comes from caring: caring enough to want the best for the audience, caring enough to take the time to really prepare a good speech, caring enough to let it show.

Follow these rules. It will make you a better speaker. It will make you a better person.

HOW TO QUICKLY IMPROVE AS A SPEAKER

The only real way to get better as a speaker is to get up and speak to an audience. Since you probably don't have a lot of opportunities to do this, here are a few tips to keep in mind when developing your speeches and presentations:

> *Get to the point*   Why waste other people's time? Why prolong your agony? I can't imagine many people complaining that a presentation was too short, unless it was a great presentation.

Say only what needs to be said For the most part, you will do just fine if you state the problem or purpose, provide some scope of it (i.e. bring in some facts, figures, and sources), propose the solution, add the benefits (and evidence that supports your proposition), and urge the audience to act.

Use fewer words The longer you are up there, the more chances you have of making mistakes. There's a lot to be said about saying less.

Do your research Don't simply state your opinion. Back it up with an expert's opinion or some statistics from a credible source. Vague references like "studies show" or "they say" is the quickest way to developing a weak speech.

Say "thank you" when you're done The audience appreciates gratitude, and a cue to begin clapping.

Franklin D. Roosevelt said it best: "Be sincere; be brief; be seated."

WHAT MAKES A GOOD SPEECH 'GOOD?'

I had a student once who got up to speak and instead of delivering a speech, he rambled for about fifteen minutes on a variety of topics that seemed to revolve around his bitterness toward his job, his recent divorce, and his aching knee. I pulled him aside after class and told him that his speech needed a lot of work. He looked at me with shock and amazement. It dawned on me that he felt he did a wonderful job because he spoke for such a long time.

That brings up an excellent question: how do we know when a speech is a good speech?

That's a really good question. I've heard students murmur to each other on particularly good speeches. It usually doesn't involve much more than a "That was really good" whisper to someone sitting nearby, and I'm sure if I pressed the issue, it would be a struggle to determine exactly why the speech was so good. There just aren't a lot of measures.

So, what can you use to measure a speech? That's where the problems begin. Time seems to be an easy route to take. Being that we have a "more is better" attitude, the longer the speech is, the better the speech is. Right?

Looking at the evidence, Lincoln's Gettysburg Address, which was only 246 words and ran about five minutes long, was a dismal speech. And, by this definition, my student's fifteen minute diatribe was sheer brilliance. So, we can already see that this isn't a good measure.

What else can be measured? How about the number of "ums?" Maybe, but that seems awfully judgmental. Instead, let's ask some simple questions about the speech itself. Then, we can add some bonus points to the delivery.

Content

Whether you are developing a speech or taking in a presentation, here are a few questions to ask to determine how good a speech is:

Was the message (or intent) clear?

Did the speaker establish in the introduction the intent of the speech and outline the major points to be covered? If you don't know what the point of the speech is within the first few minutes of the speech, then the speech is in serious trouble.

Was the message concise?

I'm all for speeches that take into consideration the necessity to set the stage or to develop particular ideas in-depth, but is there a point to what is being said? If you hear segments of a speech that seem like filler or that seem irrelevant to the point or topic, then the quality of the speech has diminished. You can begin to suspect that the speaker thinks that time spent is the mark of a good speech (which, of course, you now know better!).

Was the message helpful?

For an informative speech, did you actually learn something useful? For a persuasive speech, did it make you want to believe the speaker or do as the speaker urged? If not, then what was missing? Do you need more information? Better arguments for or against?

Delivery

Looking at the content tells us a lot about the preparation involved in the speech, but the second part of a speech is the delivery. And, yes, it's tempting to say a speech was terrible based on the "ums" and "you knows" and the stutters and the hand-wringing. But, is that entirely fair? Even if you are judging your own speech, don't you think you ought to give the speaker some credit for even getting up there?

Instead of counting the "ums" or how many times the speaker cleared his throat, let's focus on some more general impressions:

Did the speaker care about the message?

This is a judgment call. It may be a catch in the speaker's voice. It may be in the furrow of a brow. It may be the language of the speech or the intensity of the moment. It's difficult to determine, and it's often personal to each listener. But, if you feel like the speaker really cares, then there's something going right. And, that will make the speech a better one.

Did the speaker make me care about the message?

Maybe the speaker was too nervous to show a lot of emotion other than an ambient level of fear, but did the speech make you care a little more about the topic? Did you feel excited or at least mildly interested in the topic? If so, what was it that made it interesting? Again, this could be anything from the way the speaker spoke, the words chosen, the arguments presented, the gleam in the speaker's eye, or the context in which you heard the speech. Whatever it was, it worked.

Apply What You Demand

Since you now realize that there are several key elements to a good speech, ask yourself how you can place them into your own speech. There's really no secret to it. It's a formula that you use to judge other speeches. Use it to develop your own. Craft a clear message, cut down the words used to convey the message, make the message worth listening to (make it useful and do your research), and deliver it with some feeling. Put it all together and you will have a pretty good speech.

HOW LONG SHOULD A SPEECH BE?

I think the question often hidden behind that one is: how long do I have to stand up there and suffer? Three minutes? Five minutes? Ten minutes?!

Here's the thing: a bad speech is always too long, even if it lasts only a minute. That's one minute of life stolen from the audience. They'll never get it back, and they have every right to be upset. When you listen to a good speech, you often find yourself a little disappointed that it's over. When it's a bad speech, it can't end soon enough.

So, perhaps a better question to ask is not how long should a speech be, but how good should a speech be?

Time Is Not On Your Side

The problem with thinking about the time is that it makes the experience all the more excruciating. You might prepare a speech that will last five minutes, and it does when you practice in front of the mirror. You speak slowly, pause often to let ideas sink in, and you figure in a minute or two for questions at the end of the speech. Then you get up there and race through it in about one minute and thirty seconds flat. No one asks a question, and you're left up there with a nice bead of sweat trickling down your forehead.

The other problem is that you fill up the time, but to do so, you have to add a seemingly endless stream of facts that may or may not apply to the topic. Or worse, you actually ramble on for 15-20 minutes about whatever thoughts cross your mind. You walk away thinking that you did a great job because you were up there for so long.

Making people suffer for an extended period of time is dangerously close to cruel and unusual punishment.

Give Them Steak... and Only Steak

Imagine a good speech is like a good steak. You can practically hear the sizzle and it makes your mouth just water. Even if it's a small cut (the filet Mignon), you have no problem with it because it's a delicious steak. A good speech is no different. The length (amount) of the speech is not the issue as long as it is good.

But, some people insist that the speech is too short and say, "I need to add some more crap to it to make it longer." What happens if you add a piece of poop onto a steak? Yes, congratulations, you've turned that entire steak into crap. You've ruined what could have been a good steak. By adding this extra "crap" to your speech, you've ruined the whole thing. All this so you could add a few minutes to a speech. You haven't added value; you've only wasted time.

The Value of Focus

Again, the biggest issue is with mindset. You are thinking about how much time you have to be up there. Instead, you need to think about how much time you need to provide some value to the audience. When you look at it this way, it makes time much more scarce and much more precious. You don't have forever, so you need to make sure to make the most of the moment.

With this new mindset, you can now focus more on providing useful information or more powerful arguments to further your agenda (i.e. the purpose of your speech). If you want to convince us to vote for a particular candidate, what arguments or information will you need that will have the biggest potential impact upon us? If you want to teach us how to play guitar, what information will you need to get us playing by the end of the speech? Will you have enough time to accomplish this?

Notice that in these examples, you now can focus on only what's important. For the persuasive speech designed to get us to vote for a candidate, we don't need information regarding where she's from or what hobbies she has. We need information that will help us decide that she's the best qualified candidate. Anything else is a waste of time. Likewise, teaching us to play guitar is an extremely ambitious goal. In fact, you probably don't have enough time to teach us in one speech. Or, you'll have to choose one particular aspect (how to strum, play a G-chord, the basics of songwriting) so that you have a better chance of success.

Take More Time Before You Speak

A good speech is extremely focused, so the length of time is not a concern… during the speech. It's the amount of time spent preparing the speech that should be in question. Notice above that you need to ask yourself if you have enough time to accomplish your speaking goal. This question applies equally to the time spent giving the speech and the time spent preparing the speech.

You will spend a lot more time preparing the speech than you will giving the speech. The more time you prepare (i.e. researching the topic, developing the arguments or providing the information, choosing your words, tweaking the delivery, etc.), the better the quality of the speech. You may even find that you will be looking for ways to shorten the speech rather than making it longer.

No one ever gave a good speech that was too long, and every bad speech given couldn't end soon enough. If you don't have anything useful to provide the audience, the best part of your speech will be when you break Rule #2 and say, "That's it." Every second will feel like an hour, for you and for the audience. But, if you take the time before the speech to consider the needs of the audience, and then focus on the quality of the speech, you will never be up there too long. They might even ask you to cook up another steak.

JUST ONE THING

All you need is one good idea that can make a difference to someone else. If you have that, then you have the one thing you need to give a good speech.

Poor Assumptions — Poor Performance

We waste so much time dreading the idea of preparing or presenting a speech. Why? It's because we develop and deliver speeches we would hate to have to sit through. Knowing that, it's an easy leap to assume that others will probably be bored by the same things, yet that's exactly what we deliver.

We incorrectly assume that a good speech is *long*.

Wrong!

How many people walk away from a presentation thinking that an additional 20 minutes of fluff would have made that speech better? Abraham Lincoln's Gettysburg Address only took a couple of minutes to deliver, and it is still one of the greatest American speeches ever composed. I'll go out on a limb and say: no one is ever upset with a speaker getting to the point quickly.

We incorrectly assume that a good speech must be very detailed.

Wrong!

While it is important that the audience understand the topic you deliver, there is no point in getting too specific. Details will be long forgotten, but the overall sense of the topic will be retained. Details can be examined later. A speaker has only so much time to get the main ideas out there. Added details will only insure that the audience will not remember anything important and will probably walk away frustrated by the experience.

We incorrectly assume that a good speech is excessively formal. Wrong!

We create this atmosphere of formality: suits and podiums and distance between the audience and the speaker. Then, we wonder why we feel so isolated, so... on display. There's an unspoken barrier that allows the audience to comfortably ignore the speaker or sit quietly and not feel particularly engaged. There's no connection where there should be.

Provide Just One Thing

Instead, I urge you to think of just one thing that could be of use to an audience, and build your speech around that. Describe it, show us how to do it or acquire it, list the benefits of it– whatever it takes.

How? Keep in mind the elements of a good speech. Good speeches are:

Relevant Provide something that the audience can keep or use that will benefit their lives in some way, great or small

Simple Give the audience the opportunity to understand the idea from a broader perspective and give them access to the details for later study

Actionable Allow the audience the opportunity to act on the idea by giving them a clear set of steps to take

Inspiring Urge the audience to act by showing them the benefits of implementing the idea

If your speech has these four elements, you will certainly have a great speech. You won't need to add anything more. The audience will connect with you because you are providing something to them that is useful, easy to understand and implement, and feels right coming from you. Why? Because they sense that you have their best interests in mind.

And, you do. That's all it takes: just one thing.

CHAPTER 2

AUDIENCES AND TOPICS

THE AUDIENCE: WHAT IT'S ALL ABOUT

Plain and simple: It's not about you; it's all about them. The audience is your main concern. They are listening to you, but they are thinking about themselves. "Why am I listening to this? What's in it for me?"

These are fair questions, and you'd better have some real good answers.

Ultimately, audiences are self-centered. They only want to listen to what is interesting to them. And, what are audiences interested in? Themselves!

The more time you focus on yourself, the more quickly you will lose the audience. It's just like having a conversation with a self-centered person. Ever find yourself in that situation? Notice that no matter what you say, she will find a way to bring it back to herself. "You hurt your foot? You know I hurt my leg the other week doing blah blah blah…"

The conversation gets boring very quickly when everything somehow pertains to her.

However, if she were to ask you about how you hurt yourself, it becomes a little more fun for you, especially if there are any follow-up questions. "Oh, playing hockey? Wow! That sounds like a fun sport. How long have you played? Where do you play? What's your favorite team?"

You'll notice that in this conversation, she's making it all about you. Do the same for your audience, and they will always be interested in what you have to say.

KNOW YOUR AUDIENCE

How can you really know your audience? Audiences are made up of individuals who come from all walks of life, each with a set of hopes and wants. There's no real way to know each of them and be able to address and appeal to each member. Or, is there?

While you can't ever get at each individual before a speech, it helps to understand some basics of all individuals that make up an audience.

"They Are Who We Thought They Were!" (with apologies to Coach Denny Green)

To really know the audience, you can create your audience, and then develop a message catered to them. Instead of worrying about what the audience will be like, just make up one (e.g. shopping moms looking for the best deals, at-risk teens who need your message of hope). Saves time. Saves worry. (We'll talk more about how later.)

This sounds good in theory, but in practice, it's a bit different. You still have to deal with the psychology of the audience. So, while you'd love to create an audience of people who love to hear you speak and who never question your authority, it just doesn't work that way.

Here's how it goes.

All Audiences Are...

Self-centered That's right. Audiences care about themselves as individuals. They want information that will be a benefit to them. They don't care about you; they don't care about the guy sitting next to them. This is not to say that they harbor ill will toward others or that they will act in a selfish manner that could harm others. They just simply want to know why they are listening to the speech. "What's in it for me?" they ask each time someone has something to say (or sell).

This is why speakers need to spend a lot of time developing the topic and finding the meaning or utility for the audience. It takes longer (more thinking, planning, and research), but it's the only way to appeal to the audience.

Part-time listeners Attention spans waver in and out. Random thoughts ("Should I have steak for dinner or cereal?") float into their heads. Text messages buzz in and click out at dizzying rates. And, they don't remember things as well as they used to. When Homer (the poet, not Simpson) composed the Iliad and the Odyssey, he did so without the benefit of writing them down. Imagine that. I can't even get groceries without a list, otherwise I will certainly forget to buy the toothpaste (the very reason I decided to get groceries).

This is why speakers need to make use of formatting, transitions, and repetition. It sounds like you're overly repetitive when you preview the main points and then say, "Next, let's look at…" and say the main point over again. But, in light of the fact that several members of the audience just returned from whatever daydream or were listing off items to grab on the way home and feel a bit lost, this is much appreciated.

Generally friendly Okay, maybe this one is a bit of a stretch, but it will help you face them if you decide to believe me. Audiences can turn on you and will if they sense you are not working in their best interests or if you act like you are somehow better than them. You will almost definitely have a fractured audience if the topic is controversial (e.g. abortion, stem cell research, same sex marriage). But, in general, audiences are typically friendly (if a little bored or apprehensive). Remember, people don't carry around bags of overripe tomatoes to throw at a speaker if he or she fails to entertain (at least I hope they don't!).

The Exception

Obviously, if you know ahead of time who you are addressing (members of your board of directors, fellow classmates five weeks into a semester, etc.), then you probably have a good idea of your audience. If you don't, then go back to what I generally give as the best advice for almost anything: do your research.

If your group is small enough that you can get to know them personally or find out about them from interviews or public records, then do it. Knowing what they want is half the battle. Providing it to them in an efficient and elegant manner is the other half.

Know Thyself

The best way to really know how the audience will act or react or interact with the speaker is to be a member of an audience (which I'm sure you have plenty of experience with). Think about what happens to you while listening to a speech. Do you wonder if the speaker is catering to your wants or needs? Do you have random thoughts pop into your head? Did you remember to text your husband and remind him to get dental floss? What was the speaker saying about what now?

You see? You probably have as much difficulty concentrating throughout as anyone else in the audience. You aren't trying to not pay attention; you just get distracted here and there. So do they.

Audiences aren't hostile; they're just people with a lot of distractions. They have a lot on their minds. But, they aren't bad people. So, recognize that and find ways to provide them what they need in a way that helps them stay focused.

WHAT'S THE POINT?

Ever listen to a speech that had you scratching your head and asking, "What was that supposed to be about?" Are you guilty of giving this very same speech? What's going on here?

Every speech has some point to it. The question is: what's the point? Once you discover that, you can quickly determine whether or not you have a good speech.

So, What *Is* the Point?

When you are developing a speech, what is your motivation? Typical answers for me seem to revolve around the fact that I, as the instructor, have assigned the speech to the student. That's the only motivation. This may be true for someone in the workforce asked to present a report before a board committee.

If that's the case, more often than not, the point will be: *to get through the speech as quickly as possible!*

With that as the point of the speech, the audience is not a consideration. The result will be a speech that will, at best, slightly bore a polite audience. They will ask themselves, "What was the point of that?" Of course, you already know the answer... and maybe they do, too.

Service with a Smile

We could probably list several other points (such as a need for attention, though that might be a bit rare), but the true point of giving a speech has to be centered on the audience.

We speak to an audience to provide something of value to the audience.

Giving an informative speech? The point is to provide useful information for the audience? Trying to persuade them? The point is to change the audience for their improvement (or else provide valid reasons for change to benefit the audience). Giving a toast or a commemorative speech? The point is to make the occasion feel special for the audience.

I think you get the idea. It's all about them.

A Better Question, A Better Way

So, maybe a better question to ask is not "What's the point?" but rather, "Who's the point?"

Make it about them. Make it for them. That's the point.

CHOOSING A TOPIC
Something to Talk About

It's pretty simple when someone hands you a project and expects a presentation or when an instructor asks for a five-minute speech on the pros and cons of Keynesian Economic policy, but what happens when you are simply asked to develop your own topic? It's great to have all restrictions taken away at first, but then you're left with that feeling of not knowing where to begin.

So, what can you do to choose a topic to develop? We'll look at some conventional methods, but we'll have to explore why these methods are somewhat ineffective. However, I'll suggest a few simple ideas that will help by creating the audience, being the audience, and by letting the topic choose you.

The Old-fashioned Way

First, let's look at the more tried and true methods (more like "tired" and true). First, you can choose a topic you already know. A lot of my students over the years have whipped up the old "about-my-job" speech to the inaudible sighs and groans of the audience. This seems like a good idea because it can be done quickly and easily, but the problem is that you are often terrified of the audience being bored or upset with you. This is ultimately self-fulfilling; if you write a boring speech, the audience will be bored.

This raises the question: what is boring? Some people might find the subject of military strategy fascinating while others look skyward and wonder, "why me?" Fair enough, but here's the deal with audiences: they are always interested in themselves. So, when you choose a topic like "horses" or "my favorite movie," audiences will immediately ask, "Why am I listening? What's in it for me?" If your response is "nothing," then you will have a very bored or upset audience on your hands.

There are other ways to choose topics that lie among the more conventional path. These include choosing a topic you want to learn more about. This is a great way to improve yourself, and your interest in the topic increases the likelihood that others may be interested, but once again, it's tough to tell. The same goes for choosing a topic for which you have a great deal of passion. These may be the more controversial topics, such as abortion or government intervention. While you may be on fire about the subject, others might not. Or worse, you might find that they completely disagree and are now upset with you for bringing it up! Of course, an upset audience isn't bad necessarily a bad thing, but if you are already terrified of the audience, imagine an angry one!

Is there any other way? How can we create a situation that will lead to success? The answer is quite simple, yet a bit surprising: by creating a successful situation. That is accomplished by the previously mentioned strategies: creating the audience, being the audience, and by letting the topic choose you.

Create an Audience

I have students ask me what topic to develop all the time. The problem they run into is that the audience might not like their topics. My response is, "Create an audience that will be interested." They are often stuck in the belief that they are only speaking to a group of students who could care less about the speech, and essentially they are correct. That's the audience they created in their minds and that's what makes the speech such a painful process. It's tough to talk to people who don't want to talk to you. But, it's easy to talk to people who want to hear what you say. Why not create that kind of an audience?

It's really easier than you think. If you give a best man or maid of honor speech to a group of students in a class room, no one listening will look at you in confusion. They get it. You are speaking to a particular kind of audience, and the people listening will willingly suspend disbelief. In other words, no one is going to shout at you and say, "Hey, this is a classroom, not a wedding reception!" The audience will simply imagine themselves at a reception listening to your speech. You have just created an audience. More on this later; I promise—and no, I'm not stalling!

Be the Audience

This is just simply walking a mile in another person's shoes. That is, imagine yourself as a member of the audience. What would you want to listen to? What would you want to know? Imagine that the speaker (who will be you eventually) knows everything and has granted you one question, what would you want to know? Would it be how to make a million dollars? Would it be how to find a great job? Would it be where the best places to go to eat in Chicago? Chances are, other people want many of the same things. Pick one of those things and provide it to the audience. Believe me; if you can teach me how to make millions of dollars, I am going to listen very carefully!

Let the Topic Choose You

By simply creating an audience or by being the audience, the topics will come to you. Rather than trying to brainstorm a bunch of ideas or searching through blogs for a neat idea, the topics will simply appear out of sheer necessity. You won't need to talk about things that aren't important because there are so many more important things out there to discuss. Knowing what's important for the audience (or by showing the audience how something is important to them) is the real battle. After that, the topics pretty much set themselves.

Putting It All Together

Creating an audience, being the audience, and letting topics choose you are really ways of essentially stacking the deck. You are giving yourself a greater chance to succeed by creating a situation that allows you to be successful. When you create the situation, you get to control the situation.

I'm not suggesting that this is an easier method of choosing a topic. However, it is a more thoughtful method. It keeps in mind the needs of the audience. Remember that the audience wants to know what's in it for them. The initial topic might sound boring or useless at first, but that's where you show them how it is useful.

Ultimately, it's really all about them. It's only when you forget about your needs (such as the need to not feel frightened by an audience, or the need to choose a topic to get the speech over with already!) and focus on the needs of the audience that you will choose better topics and achieve greater success as a speaker.

PROVIDE RELEVANCE TO THE TOPIC

Choosing a topic for a speech can be the most difficult part of developing a speech. If only you had some basic direction in which to go. Of course, a good way to start is to read the previous section on choosing a topic, but there's something more you might need to consider: relevance.

Do you ever wonder why you get so nervous speaking to an audience? You might have a lot of ideas, but they usually center on the audience feeling somewhat annoyed with you up there talking to them. It's almost assumed that the audience is this somewhat passive aggressive group of flinty-eyed individuals that stare at you in anger and boredom, just polite enough not to say anything, but certainly not nice enough to encourage you.

But, why is that? Again, it can be boiled down to one word: relevance.

Perception Is Reality

If you think an audience is upset with your speech, you may or may not be correct. You can't know what other people are thinking. But, you can guess, and it's usually based on something within you. Perhaps you've been bored and irritated with others giving speeches, and the main reason is that the topic of the speech seemed completely irrelevant to you.

So, you write a completely irrelevant speech and then get up there and wonder why you feel so nervous…

Of course you feel nervous! You should!

Well, you shouldn't have to, but that's because there's an easy fix.

Make the Topic Relevant

That's right. You can discuss almost any topic you want if you can make or prove it useful to the audience. How do you do that?

Think about your topic. What will the audience be able to do with the information you've given them? If you don't know, then they won't either. So, as you develop your topic, provide a concrete purpose by filling in the following:

After this speech, the audience will be able to _____.

Let's say you want to discuss money or finances. That's an awfully broad topic. What is your purpose? If you say that your purpose is to help people understand how money and banking work, you might narrow it down, but what can people do with that knowledge? More often than not, they will simply shrug and get busy forgetting what you said.

But, if you give it a more concrete purpose, that is, something they can actually do with that information, they will more likely remember what you said and act on it. They will also listen more intently. They may even jot a few things down to remind them what to do with the information later.

You know you have a good speech on your hands when people are sitting up and taking notes.

Relevance Is Actionable

If there's one thing to remember that will immediately improve the quality of your speeches and that will help you to feel less nervous while addressing an audience, it's that you must make the topic relevant. The best way to make a topic relevant is to make it actionable. Give the audience information they can use—a step-by-step set of instructions, a plan, data that will help lead to a decision, or anything that they will be able to use to their benefit.

When an audience can see how to use the information you provide, they will be much more interested in what you have to say. Once you know that, you'll notice that your nervousness will simply disappear.

CREATE THE AUDIENCE TO CREATE THE MESSAGE

See, I told you we'd eventually get here!

You are trying to develop a topic, but you have no idea what to say. Or, you have a topic, but you have no idea who will be listening. Or, you know who will be listening, but you don't know what they'll think. No wonder you're terrified.

When you talk to your friends, you feel comfortable. You have a set of expectations of how they'll react to things you might say. I assume they are your friends because these expectations are generally positive and supportive.

However, an audience feels like a great unknown, and what is more terrifying than the unknown? If only there was a way ahead of time to determine who you were speaking to, or how they would react to your topic.

May I humbly suggest that you create an audience rather than try to cater to an unknown audience?

You Already Do It

Whether you are aware of it or not, you engage in a process of creating an audience every time you prepare a speech. Unfortunately, a monster is the result. Rather than creating an audience filled with individuals who want or need the message you bring, you are facing down a group of people who are either slightly bored or generally annoyed with you, the message, or the venue. Is this true?

Well, yes, it is, if you have that expectation. If you create that audience, then that's what you face.

Truthfully, we can never really know the internal state of another person. You never really know what someone is thinking. All you have is what you see, and what you think they are thinking. A blank expression can be interpreted any way you want. Your expectation colors your perception. If you think someone is annoyed with you, any expression or lack of expression is interpreted as annoyance. And, you could be right. But, you could also be wrong.

Start With What They Need

Why do that to yourself? Instead, create an audience. Think about what an audience would need or want. Start with what you would need or want. Do you need more money for retirement? Do you want to know what to do if you're stranded on the side of a road with no cell phone signal?

Think broadly of your basic needs and then try to figure out how you could accomplish that. For example, how could you get more money for retirement? Develop a savings plan. Contribute to a 401k plan. Learn to invest in the markets. Each of these ideas can become full presentations on their own.

Once you determine your needs or wants, you can probably guess that others will have a similar set of needs. Not sure? Then do some research. How much does the average person have in savings? What's the median income in your industry? How many people at your company contribute to a 401k plan?

Once you determine this, you'll have a better idea of how many people need this kind of information. Develop your message accordingly.

Project the Proper Attitude

Now comes the hard part. When you look out into the audience, what do you see? Most likely, all of your fears and doubts. You project them onto a group of people and it becomes an outward manifestation of your own issues. If you are bored with your topic, you assume others will be bored, too. But, if you are excited about your topic, it's possible others will be excited, too.

Since you've prepared this presentation for an audience that wants or needs this information, assume that the audience before you is made up of exactly those people. Will there be people who really don't care? Maybe, but how will you truly know? If you believe that everyone can benefit from what you have to say, then say it like you mean it and believe that the audience is there to receive it.

In short, when you talk to people who want to listen, it's a much easier task than dealing with people who don't want to bother. Since you don't know what people are really thinking or feeling, project a group of people who need what you have to offer. Make sure your message provides for them what they need, and you will surely be in a much better situation. Don't make it any harder than it has to be. Create a presentation worth listening to and then create an audience that wants to listen. You'll find public speaking much easier and far more gratifying that way.

INSPIRE THE AUDIENCE

What do you honestly consider a good speech? No, I don't mean in reference to your own speeches. When you sit down to listen to a speaker in a meeting or a seminar or at some semi-formal function, what are your expectations?

Maybe you want the speaker to be engaging, funny, relevant, or at least brief.

Or, maybe (to paraphrase a line from the movie Jerry McGuire) you just want to be inspired.

That's fair. Just one question: why aren't you holding yourself to that standard?

Magic in the Message

Maybe you just don't know how to inspire an audience. Maybe you are too worried about getting all the facts out there, checking all of your sources, making clear arguments. Or, maybe you have focused too much on how terrified you are to speak to an audience, let alone attempt to make them feel anything.

But, that's just it; what's the point of getting up there and addressing an audience if not to make them feel something? More than that, why make them feel bad with a message of gloom or doom? There's enough bad news out there that's widely circulated and widely known. Why add to that?

You don't realize that there's magic in the message. You just have to bring it to them.

How to Inspire

The hardest way to try to learn to inspire an audience is to listen to great speakers give great speeches and try to copy them. Some speakers had the perfect message for the perfect audience at the perfect time, thus securing their place in history. That might be asking a bit much of us. But, there are some things you can do that will help:

Provide a sense of hope One of the reasons the Star Trek franchise has enjoyed such enduring success is its overall message of hope for the future. Robots trying to destroy humanity or humans enslaved in some sort of tyrannical social order make for gripping tales, but they often leave audiences feeling a bit bummed out. Your message needs to give the audience a sense that the future can and will get brighter if we work toward that. Otherwise, what's the point of listening to your message? What's the point of anything if there's nothing to hope for?

Make it personal Give that sense of hope to each individual. Make the solution to the problem something that is accessible to each person in the audience. They need to feel that the message is relevant to all, but especially to each. When a person feels he has an opportunity to make a positive impact great or small, he will likely feel inspired.

Be true As much as you want to provide hope, make sure that the message is true. Discuss the problem realistically. Discuss the solution realistically. Discuss the benefits realistically. It has to ring true; otherwise, the audience will not connect with your message.

Believe in the message Inspiration is sparked by faith. Believe in what you have to say with absolute conviction, and speak with a passion that can only come from this belief. Others will follow.

I suppose choosing your words carefully, or choosing the right venue will increase the likelihood of inspiring an audience. But, it ultimately comes down to the positive empowerment your message provides, and the strength with which you carry the belief in that message. Do you want to inspire an audience? Then give them every reason to feel inspired. Expect nothing less from any speaker, including you.

LIVES ARE AT STAKE: FRAMING THE IMPORTANCE OF THE MESSAGE

You have to give a sales presentation next week or report last quarter's earnings to a committee for strategic planning purposes. You've been there before and you'll be there again, but it doesn't make it any less stressful. Sure, you try to be as persuasive as possible given the context, or you try to make the information as interesting as possible, but how interesting can numbers be?

Here's where you need to reframe how you think of the information or the intent: Lives are at stake, and what you have to say can save them.

You have to take into your topic the thought that what you have to say is of the utmost importance. If you don't think it's important, then why will the audience? If it's not important, then why bother listening?

These are fair questions and you must spend time addressing them (yes, even in the speech or presentation).

Is It Really Important?

Once you think of what you have to do or say as important, even life-saving, the next step is to show us how. Don't just say it's really, really important. Say it like you mean it. Look like you mean it. Act like you mean it. Actually mean it! Then, prove it.

Give us some evidence that the topic will have some benefit in our lives. Give us numbers, scenarios, sources, testimony. Show us that you care not only in your actions and in your words, but with the sheer amount of preparation put into what you have to say. Once we see the connection to us (that is how the information impacts us and that you are here for our benefit), we are more apt to listen and listen more intently.

So, back to the sales scenario mentioned earlier: do you believe the product you sell is a benefit to the potential customers? Why do you believe this? What evidence do you have to support this belief? Why should I believe you?

For the strategic planning committee: what are these numbers showing us in terms of how the company performed? Is this part of a larger issue? What can be said about what the future holds based on the relevant data? How does this affect the company?

By the way, you can often ask these questions as part of your presentation. Some answers or suggestions can come from you, and some can come from them.

Reframing to Overcome Nerves

Incidentally, seeing the importance of your topic (i.e. reframing) is a great way to overcome nervousness. Think about that for a minute. Imagine having to give a speech and thinking, "No one here really cares about me or what I have to say, so I shouldn't even bother." You probably have thought that very thing. What you had to say just didn't seem all that important, even if it was.

Now imagine you see someone choking. You immediately recognize that her life is in danger. Do you think, "I wonder if she even cares about me or that I know the Heimlich maneuver? Should I even bother?"

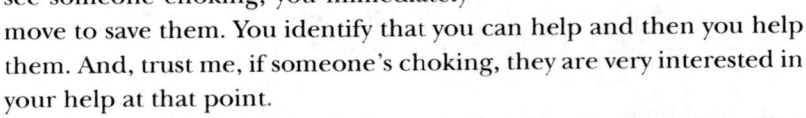

Clearly this is a silly scenario. If you see someone choking, you immediately move to save them. You identify that you can help and then you help them. And, trust me, if someone's choking, they are very interested in your help at that point.

It's the same concept in giving a speech or presentation. The audience is dying for your help, only they aren't aware of it. You have to show them that they are choking, and that you have the life-saving techniques, and then offer to be of assistance.

It's a lot of work, and it requires that you forget about your personal issues (i.e. your fear of addressing audiences), but it's that important. You can save lives (or make them better), but only if you see that way. When you accept that your message is life-saving, you'll find that your speeches will be much more passionate and your attitude much more compassionate—two elements of a great speaker. Speak to an audience. Speak for an audience. Then they will always be willing to listen.

QUESTIONS TO ASK, COMMENTS TO KEEP

So, as mentioned, lives are at stake, and the message (i.e. your speech or presentation) can save them. That's a great way to develop a topic. I also mentioned that it can help you to overcome nerves. Just realizing the importance of what you want to accomplish makes it easier to get up there and speak.

But, sometimes it's difficult to remember that when you are faced with actually delivering your speech. And, as terrifying as it may seem to be speaking, sometimes it's even worse just before you go up to speak. The anticipation can be worse than the realization. You're just sitting there, thinking about what's going to happen and (worse!) what might happen.

This is when you need someone or something to remind you what you are trying to accomplish. And, yes, I will be too happy to provide that for you– a few simple questions to ask yourself, and a few simple comments to remember that your nervousness is not as important as the message.

Questions to Ask

Are you too nervous to talk to a friend?

I can certainly understand a little trepidation when approaching a stranger. I can certainly understand the fear that washes over you when facing a whole audience of strangers. But, what if these people were your friends? Would you feel less nervous? My guess is that you would be a lot more willing to talk to people you considered friends over people you considered strangers.

Why not consider them your friends? About the only thing you have to do to think of them as friends is to care about them. And that leads into the second question...

Are you too nervous to care?

Hey, these are your friends we're talking about. Caring and nervousness only go together when it involves you. When it involves others, caring is a very comforting feeling. It gives you the strength and courage you need to do what must be done: save lives—through public speaking!

Are you too nervous to save a life?

We talked about this before; if you see someone choking and you know the Heimlich maneuver, I think it's time to act. It's not time to reflect on whether or not the choking person thinks you're cool. If you have the means to save a life, would you sit and worry about how people feel about you? Isn't it more important to save lives first, and then worry about whether or not the people think you are cool?

If your ego is more important than the well-being of others, then how can you ever hope to be successful in business or life? Business is people. Life is people. Helping others is the key to success in both. There's no time to worry about how silly you think you look or how scared you feel.

Comments to Keep

You may have noticed that each question builds upon itself. Through a few simple questions, you've transformed the audience from strangers to friends, and you've transformed yourself from someone who cares more about them than yourself. Good for you, but somehow we've turned this into something about us again, and we need to remind ourselves that it's really not about us.

To that, here are a few simple comments that you can repeat in order to help you refocus on what's important: them.

1. It's not about you.

It's about helping others (what I've dramatically referred to as "saving lives"). Forget about yourself. Forget about what others may think about you. Forget about what you may think about you. It's really not about you. Accept that and move on to what it's about…

2. It's about the message.

You have a message that will change people for the better. They will have information that will help them make better decisions or gain skills that will improve their lives, even just a little bit. That message will give them confidence and hope in uncertain times. They will be happier and healthier as a result of the message.

3. It's all about "them."

Notice how often "they" get mentioned? When you wonder who "they" are, "they" are "them"—the audience. As important as the message is, it's really all about the audience. Messages come from many sources, and they say many things. But, they lose all significance without the audience. There can be no impact without the audience. It's all about them.

So, just before you face the audience, face down your fear by remembering what it is you are trying to do: bring a positive message to an audience in need. It's that important. They are that important.

CHAPTER 3

BUILDING THE SPEECH

THE IMPORTANCE OF THE INTRODUCTION

If there's one thing I tend to stress in the development of a speech, it's the introduction. "Why?" you may ask. Good question! The introduction is the hardest part of a speech in terms of preparation. You've got the topic, you've done the research, and you know what needs to be said, but you just don't know where to start.

The best way to start is by understanding the point of an introduction.

Introductions set the tone, give us a purpose, and outline the game plan. There's always more, but let's start there.

Setting the Tone—Are You a Good Speech or a Bad Speech?

Life would be a lot easier if a speech could start with something simple, such as:

> *"I'm going to show you how to lower your taxes. Okay? Ready? Go."*

I suppose that's very clear, and there may be something to be said for that. But, much like getting a gift, half the fun is in the anticipation of the gift. Yes, I'm talking about the wrapping paper. A good timely example is buying an Apple product. Apple puts a lot of time into the experience of opening their product. Some people actually film it. We look forward to what's inside, even if it's a pair of socks. Handing me a pair of socks, while appreciated, seems less fun somehow without the gift wrapping and presentation. A good introduction does just that: it gets us excited about the speech.

Spend some time getting us interested in the topic. How does what you have to say affect us? Are you teaching us a skill? If so, indicate to us how useful this skill will be. Will it make us lots of money? Will we be able to impress or entertain friends? Will we achieve some sort of inner peace?

Are you trying to convince us to do something or believe something? If so, what's the potential price of not listening to you? Returning to the example about lowering taxes, perhaps you could try to convince us to go with your tax preparation service. Tell us how much people pay in taxes every year (and the source of that information) or how much people pay needlessly. Then ask us, given our economic status, if we can afford to waste money like that. Now you got us listening!

Give Us Purpose—A Reason to Listen

Here's the secret: by talking about how a topic impacts us, you are already giving the speech a solid purpose. Audiences are always self-interested, so talking to them about them is always a good thing. Audiences are made up of individuals, and these individuals want to improve their lives in small and large ways. How? Answer that question, and you have a purpose.

To develop a purpose, you must determine what an audience wants or needs. While that varies from person to person, remember, almost everyone wants whatever they have to be better. This might be more money, more free time, better relationships with others. Again, it will vary from person to person, but certainly working toward the improvement of another's station will be met positively.

Outline the Game Plan—How Long Is This Speech?

You got us interested in the topic, and you have a basic idea of what you want to do. What's next? Giving us an outline (or preview) of what's to come. Much like an agenda for a meeting, this is a list of the main points that will be covered in the speech. So, to completely exhaust the example, what are the three or four steps involved in lowering our taxes?

Don't discuss them in detail; just give us a title version of what will be discussed in the speech. This does two things for us: it gives us a game plan of what to expect in the body of the speech, and it gives us an idea of how long the speech will be. Remember, an audience acts in self-interest, and no matter how useful or interesting a speech may be, the audience will forever wonder when it will end (presumably so they can get back to whatever it is they really want to do or think). Giving the audience a list of the main points allows them to get a sense for how long the speech might be.

Speeches are not as tough as you think, if you take the time to develop the introduction. In fact, with a well-developed introduction, the rest is just details. So, take the time to really develop your introductions; give the audience something interesting to listen to, something useful. Let them know what to expect along the way. The audience will appreciate the effort. I think you will, too.

CRAFTING AN INTRODUCTION

No doubt about it; the introduction will make or break a speech. Within the span of 30 seconds to a minute, the audience will know if the speech is going to be a good one or a bad one. That is, they'll know if they want to listen to it or break out their cell phones and start texting friends and family. So, you need to quickly develop a topic in a way that will get the audience interested. While there are any number of ways to do this, there is a basic formula you can use that will quickly get you into the body of your speech and allow the audience an opportunity to determine just how good or useful the presentation will be.

There are five basic elements to a good introduction: the attention getter, stating the topic/problem, credibility, impact on the audience, and (most importantly) the preview of main points.

Attention-Getter

The first thing you say or do, by definition, becomes your attention getter. This is why we spent a little time establishing Rule #1 (Never ever start with "My speech is about..."). When you start with something weak (like saying, "Okay, I'm really nervous, so be cool" or "This speech is about computers and stuff"), you are essentially admitting that your speech is not all that good. You might have some good information, but you clearly lack polish. Growing up in a world of entertainment (thanks to mass media), we like polished products. So you need to bring in something a little extra.

What exactly is that something extra? I'll leave that to you, but a few ideas include:

- ask a rhetorical question (please, not "How are you?") pertaining to the topic
- state an important fact
- use a quote
- tell an interesting story that begins to illustrate the idea of the speech

Be creative. The audience will appreciate it.

"Ever wish you could save a few hundred dollars?"

Yeah, it's that easy.

State the Topic/Problem

Once you get the attention of the audience, you need to give them some idea of where this is going. So, for example, if you got them into the speech by asking a question like "Ever wish you could save a few hundred dollars?" you have our attention, but what does this pertain to? Are you talking about how to budget money? Are you talking about shopping tips or tricks? Swindling passers-by with a shell game? This statement clears up the confusion.

> "Building your own computer can save you hundreds of dollars over purchasing a computer."

Ah! Now, you're talking. This is better than saying, "Ever think about building a computer? Well, I'll show you how." Big deal. Who cares? But, this idea of saving money sounds good, and if I have to build a computer to save some money, maybe I will. Maybe I will...

Credibility

You've got the audience's attention, and they now have some idea of what you are suggesting (in this case, building a computer). Now, you need some credibility.

You can probably state that you assemble your own computers as a hobby. That might work. But you might also consider bringing in some outside sources that let the audience know you know your stuff. In other words, do you have evidence to support the claim that building a computer is cheaper than buying one?

> "Brand X Computers states that their latest computer, the Whiz Bang Quad-Core 3.0, costs about $1,300 including shipping and handling, but looking at ComputerParts-a-Plenty's website shows that buying each part will cost you only $795 including shipping."

Yes, I realize that I'm using fake companies (to protect the innocent), but you get the idea. Use actual sources and real numbers, and you'll earn that credibility.

Impact on the Audience

Sometimes, this is built into the topic. Sometimes, it's somewhere in the credibility portion of the introduction. But, sometimes, it just needs to be stated outright:

> "So, building your own computer could save you just over $500 dollars, and in today's uncertain economy, that's a significant savings."

This would work a lot better than trying to make a claim like "Everyone needs computers, so I'll show you how to build one." First, where's the evidence that supports the claim? Does everyone really need a computer? Maybe, maybe not, but we need to know where you got your facts to support that. And second, you're making a leap from needing one to building one. Why not just buy one? Of course, the answer is: to save money! That's why you made the claim in the first place, so go back and refer to it.

The Preview Statement

This is perhaps the most important element in the introduction. It's basically a list of the main points you will cover. You can even restate the purpose. But, the important thing is that the audience gets a list of all the points you will cover.

> "To show you how to build a computer, we will consider the processor, the motherboard, memory, and storage space to help you to learn how to build a computer so you can save some serious cash."

Put It All Together

Put it all together, and you have yourself an introduction that may not be as dynamic as a professionally packaged presentation from a major ad agency or marketing firm, but you have something that will pique curiosity, show proficiency and competence, and outline a plan that can be easily followed throughout the rest of the presentation (see if you notice the little extra added into this introduction):

> "Ever wish you could save a few hundred dollars? The Census Bureau reported that median income in the U.S. was just over $50,000 in 2007, but with the stock market in turmoil, dropping to just above 7,000, down from a high of 14,000 in October of 2007, Americans are starting to feel the pinch. How can you save money when you have so little and still enjoy all the technological amenities we've come to take for granted in our

society? Let's consider the idea of saving on technology costs. In fact, building your own computer can save you hundreds of dollars over purchasing a computer. Brand X Computers' website states that their latest computer, the Whiz Bang Quad-Core 3.0 costs about $1,300 including shipping and handling, but looking at ComputerParts-a-Plenty's website shows that buying each part will cost you only $795 including shipping. So, building your own computer could save you just over $500 dollars, and in today's uncertain economy, that's a significant savings. To show you how to build a computer, we will consider the processor, the motherboard, memory, and storage space to help you to learn how to build a computer so you can save some serious cash."

Not too shabby!

Yes, a little smoothing between the major components was done, and needs to be done, but it really is a simple matter of connecting the dots. Keeping in mind the basic elements of the introduction will allow you the opportunity to build these connecting statements and ultimately a memorable introduction.

JAZZ UP THE PREVIEW

We've established that you need a preview statement that gives us the idea of the main points of discussion, but we need to look at how well you are doing that. While listening to informative speeches, audiences will want to know "what's in it for me?" That's a fair question, and the preview of main points combined with the purpose will give them just that.

But, have you made it enticing?

Jazz—Adding a Little Something Extra

Much like taking basic chords in music and adding extra notes that give it that jazzy flourish, it is important to add something extra to your preview statement to create a sense of excitement and expectation. Let's face it; you are selling something (sometimes literally) every time you give a presentation. So, you need to use words and ideas that compel people to want to buy.

Smooth Sailing with Salesmanship

Let's look at an example. Recently, a colleague of mine asked me to look at a presentation concerning some economic forecasts in the local job market. The presentation was designed to help job counselors understand the new economy, particularly the latest trend toward environmental consciousness as an industry. The preview of main points looked something like this:

> "Looking at our agenda, we'll go over the following items: projections of job growth 2009–2016, declining jobs, the new eco-friendly jobs, some recommended sources, and some next steps."

Well, it's clear, and I always appreciate that, but it lacks a certain something. It fails to captivate my interest. We need to jazz it up a bit. How about something like:

> "Today, you will be able to
> - *identify the fastest growing jobs*
> - *see which jobs to avoid*
> - *explore 'green' jobs—the hottest growing sector*
> - *learn about the 5 absolutely essential websites*
> - *get started right away with our job-finder toolkit!"*

You have the same topics, but now they seem more exciting, more useful. Maybe it's a bit over the top, but you're inevitably going to get a bit of criticism for anything you do. Would you rather be criticized for boring people or for trying to get them interested in your topic? I'll take the latter.

BUILDING THE BODY (OF THE SPEECH)

Once you've properly put together an introduction, you need to move into the body of the speech. Having crafted that introduction so well, you now have a blueprint for the body of the speech. Your preview statement will contain the main points you plan to discuss in the body of the speech. The body will be an augmentation of that preview.

As you will see, once you've figured out how to develop one of the main points, you've figured out the formula for all of the main points. It basically comes down to providing transitions between the points, augmenting the points, and formatting the points. Doing this, you might find yourself in the unique position of having more to say than you need. You will have the luxury of editing for time constraints. Let's look at all of this more closely..

Transitioning between Points

This is as simple as saying "First," "Second," "Next," or "Finally." If you want to get fancier (and help the audience out significantly), you can repeat the main points by providing a transitional summary/preview. This looks more like "Now that we've discussed _____, let's look at _____." Fill in the blanks with main points.

Augmenting the Points

Once you list the various points you plan to discuss, you have to provide some augmentation or amplification. What does that mean? It means you have to explain your point. What are you talking about? If it's an informative speech, what is involved in this step of the process? If it's persuasion, explain your argument in more detail.

Once you've explained it a little more, provide the audience with some evidence to support your point. Use examples, statistics, or testimony to help. Short quotes never hurt anybody, but don't feel like you need one for every point.

Be sure to use a credible source or two and make sure to list that source.

Finally, tell the audience what to make of the point. This is a bit vague, admittedly. But, it's still necessary. As a speaker, you are connecting dots for the audience. In an informative speech, you are helping them to see how this particular point relates to the purpose of the speech (in our earlier example, show the audience how one of the parts of a computer helps them to build a computer less expensively). For a persuasive speech, your point has to show the audience how change is necessary based on the argument provided.

Formatting the Points

While developing each main point, remember to keep them in the order listed in the preview. When you list them in that order, the audience will expect that order. Changing it up will only confuse the audience (something you never want to do).

Also, keep each main point about the same length as the previous main point. Audience members get into a rhythm when it comes to a speech, and they will try to find patterns in the speech. If the first main point is about one minute long, they'll expect the next point to be a minute long. If the first point is a minute and the second point is five minutes, the audience will wonder if the next main point will be 10 or 20 minutes. Not only that, they will begin to think that the first main point was not as important as the second main point. Or, they will get lost in the longer main point, thinking that you've covered several main points.

Follow the Formula

Speech writing is surprisingly simple, if you follow a formula. So, all you really need to do is follow the instructions below. To help a bit, let's use the same preview statement regarding computers:

> *"To show you how to build a computer, we will consider the processor, the motherboard, memory, and storage space to help you to learn how to build a computer so you can save some serious cash."*

1. Transition from Introduction to Main Point #1
- "First, let's examine... (Main Point #1)"

In this case, you'd actually say something like, "First, let's examine the processor as it pertains to building your own computer."

2. Discuss Main Point #1
- Provide explanation of step (involved in a process), idea, or argument.
- Clarify with an example/statistic/testimony.
- Add quote from trusted source or testimonial (optional).
- What are we to make of this point?

3. Transition from Main Point #1 to Main Point #2
- "Next, let's examine (Main Point #2)..." or
- "Now that we've looked at Main Point #1, let's move on to Main Point #2..."

In our example, you'd say...

> "Next let's examine the motherboard"

or

> "Now that we've looked at the processor, let's move on to the motherboard."

4. Main Point #2 (Make sure it's about the same length of time as Main Point #1)
- Explanation of the step/idea/argument.
- How is it different than Main Point #1?
- Clarify with an example/statistic/testimony.
- Add quote from trusted source or testimonial (optional).
- What are we to make of this point?

5. Transition from Main Point #2 to Main Point #3
- Third, let's look at (Main Point #3)..."
- Now that we've looked at Main Point #2, let's move on to Main Point #3...

Do I really need to spell it out again? Fine...

> "Third, let's look at the memory..."

or

> "Now that we've looked at the motherboard, let's examine the memory."

6. Main Point #3 (Make sure it's about the same length as Main Point #2)
- Explanation of the step/idea/argument.
- How is it different than Main Point #1 and Main Point #2?
- Clarify with an example/statistic/testimony.

- Add quote from trusted source or testimonial (optional).
- What are we to make of this point?

7. Transition from Main Point #3 to Main Point #4
- "Finally, let's talk about (Main Point #4)"
- "We've looked at (Main Point #1, Main Point #2, and Main Point #3), but we also need to consider (Main Point #4)."

You can pretty much repeat this process for as many main points as you have (though I'd set a limit at around five main points).

"Finally let's talk about storage."

"We've looked at the processor, the motherboard, and the memory, but we also need to consider the storage."

8. Main Point #4 (Make sure it's about the same length as Main Point #3)
- Explanation of the step/idea/argument.
- How is it different than Main Point #1, Main Point #2, and Main Point #3?
- Clarify with an example/statistic/testimony.
- Add quote from trusted source or testimonial (optional).
- What are we to make of this point?

Time Is Now On Your Side (Unlike Earlier!)

Putting all of this together, you may find that you have written yourself a very extensive speech. You may actually have to consider editing your speech down to only the most essential elements. Imagine that: cutting down your speech to fit into a given time frame. That would put most speech writers on unfamiliar territory. But, believe me; it's much better to cut down a speech than to have to add to it.

I'll leave the actual work up to you. It is your speech, after all!

IN CONCLUSION, SAY SOMETHING MORE

Conclusions are tricky. If a conclusion summarizes the main points, then why not just make that the body of the speech and be done with it? How do you say something new while summarizing what you've already said? For that matter, how do you transition into it without actually saying "In conclusion...?"

All of these questions can be answered by understanding that a conclusion helps the audience see the point of the speech. So, if it's a persuasive speech, the audience will see that you went through this entire process to change the audience for their benefit. If it's an informative speech, the conclusion helps the audience see how the various points come together to provide them with a new understanding or skill set.

So, how do you construct a conclusion?

Transition into the Conclusion

I realize that saying "In conclusion..." seems a bit obvious and shows a lack of skill. Certainly, you should never write "in conclusion" in a paper. But, keep in mind that in a paper, it's much more obvious that you've reached the conclusion; there are only a few paragraphs or pages left. We can actually see the end of the paper. This is not the case for a speech.

So, I suppose you could try a variation of "in conclusion" by saying:

- *"And, so..."*
- *"As I close..."*
- *"So, what have we learned?"*

Or something like that. It works. It's not great, but it works.

Another way to signal the transition into the conclusion is a nice pause. Let that final point sink in, then move into the conclusion. It may take a second or two for the audience to realize what has happened, but once they start to hear the review of the main points, they'll know that you've moved into the conclusion.

Review the Original Problem (Purpose)

Once you've transitioned into the conclusion, you need to look at the original problem (i.e. the established need for change in persuasion or the missing skill set or lack of understanding over an issue in an informative speech). Remind the audience what this presentation was all about.

Review the Points

Take a moment to look at the main points and how they address (solve) the problem. Show them how each of the arguments leads them to conclude that change must take place or how each point gives them more complete knowledge and understanding about the given topic.

Next Steps

Once you've built your case (i.e. shown the audience how your points address the problem/purpose), tell the audience about the next course of action. For persuasion, this is an urge to action/change (e.g. "I urge you to stop using Z and switch to Product X!"). For an informative speech, this is where you invite members to take advantage of their new found skill or knowledge (e.g. "Now that you know how change your oil, you won't have to worry about the high prices of your local oil change station. You can do it yourself!")

Encouragement

Let the audience know that things will be better in the future as a result of listening to the speech, because the change or new knowledge is a good thing that will lead to positive results (if applied).

Ending the Speech

Simply say "thank you." There is no need to add much else. You've reminded them of the problem/purpose, summarized the main point, shown how the points fit together to address the problem/

purpose, you've provided the next steps, and you've encouraged them. What more needs to be said? Just "thank you."

Bringing the Meaning—Saying Something More

Remember, the conclusion is a way to wrap it all up. However, a wrap-up is not just reiterating what was already said. If you end your speech with "In conclusion, I showed you how to make a peanut butter and jelly sandwich by taking peanut butter, jelly, and bread and mixing them together. Thank you," you've missed the point of the conclusion—and by the way, please don't ever prepare a speech on how to make a peanut butter and jelly sandwich.

You need to add more than just a brief summary of the main points. Tell the audience what they mean. What does it all mean to them? What are they supposed to do or think as a result?

"We've looked at the facts. We've seen the effects on our environment. We've heard the potential consequences of not acting. It all leads to a very obvious need for us to..."

Notice how the particular facts aren't repeated. Only the bigger ideas are added as a reminder of what was said in the body of the speech. This helps the audience to see how all that stuff (facts and figures) fit together. It also keeps it brief. Adding too much detail will make it sound like you are repeating the body of the speech.

A conclusion is an opportunity for you to bring meaning to the speech. It's a synthesis of facts and arguments with the problem or purpose. You help the audience see what they couldn't or wouldn't see before. It's one last chance to have an impact on them, so choose your words carefully.

THE TAKE-AWAY

Every good speech has some broad purpose, such as to enhance understanding (informative), effect some change (persuasive), or simply to evoke some emotion (as in a special occasion). But, there's a more specific purpose to each speech that needs to be spelled out.

As an example, you might intend to inform an audience of the health problems associated with a particular product. So, what's the purpose?

I've had students tell me the purpose is stated right there: *"to inform the audience, specifically about different health problems when using a certain product... How can it be any clearer?"*

Look more carefully.

Why are you *really* informing the audience of this? What are you trying to do?

The Take-Away

I used to call it the "moral of the story." I liked that. It was nice and clear. The problem is that every speech I heard after that ended with: *"In conclusion, the moral of the story is..."*

Instead, I'll call it the "take-away." It's the same thing; I just prefer to hear people say, "What can we take away from this?" It's more appropriate, considering a moral to a story involves... well, a story, which is essentially a fictional or allegorical piece.

While a specific purpose is stated in the introduction, the take-away is that same purpose placed in the conclusion. It simply tells us what we can or should or must do as a result of listening to the speech. You can see why it's so tempting to use the term "moral." But, don't.

The True Purpose?

Given this, what is the take-away from the example earlier? Your introduction started out with the idea of informing the audience, but we can see now that you really want to persuade us not to use that product. That's your specific purpose. That's your take-away.

So, go back to your introduction, and change it from informing the audience about the health problems associated with the use of a product to something closer to your take-away. For example, to persuade them to stop using a product that can harm them.

Your speeches will be much clearer in intent and much more effective as a result.

QUESTION AS TRANSITION?

I mentioned that an easy way to transition into the conclusion was to simply say "In conclusion" or "And, so...." I also stated it wasn't a great way to transition. I also mentioned that transitions in the body of the speech could be something as easy as saying "first," "second," "next," and "finally." Or, you could add something like, "Now that we've discussed [Main Point A], let's look at [Main Point B]."

Now, there's another way to transition to the next point or (especially) into the conclusion: the question.

A Question as a Transition? Really?

How does it work? Quite smoothly, actually. Main points lead into new main points, and usually there's a train of thought that progresses logically from point to point within a speech. Since ideas logically follow each other (or should), your transition can include the implied question.

For example, notice the question that starts the last paragraph above. The preceding statement suggests that there's a new method of transitioning from one point to the next, which is using a question to transition into a new point. Reading that, the reader may ask, "A question? Really? How does that work?"

As a speaker, you can give that thought a voice by asking the question for the audience. Simply ask the question that is on their minds based on what you've just discussed as a segue into the next point. This will guide the audience into the next section very smoothly (as mentioned).

Conclusions, Too?

You may be asking, "Hey, does this work for conclusions?" (Yes, I'm using this transition device within this article to help you see it in action, so forgive the overkill.) Yes, it does work for conclusions, too.

Of course, you'll need a more sweeping question such as "Where does this leave us?" or "What can we draw from this?" This will allow you to summarize the main points and relate the purpose of the speech to the audience and urge them to take the necessary next step.

How Many Questions are Too Many Questions?

Should you transition every point using a question? I have used this device for most of my transitions here, and hopefully, you've thought to yourself that it seems a bit excessive. You would be correct.

The question transition works here and there, but be sure to mix it up a bit. Saying "First" or "Next" is a perfectly good transition, as is a sprinkled in "Let's move on to [the next Main Point]." Now, you have an added tool for the transition between points or into your conclusion.

Also, be sure to use only one transition per transition. Don't string them together into some sort of uber-transition: "And so, in conclusion, now that we've looked at these main points, what have we learned, and what are the next steps?" It's just too much!

So, where does that leave us? Enough questions, already!

EDIT FOR EFFECTIVENESS

I will listen to about 25-30 speeches in a given evening, and one thing I've consistently noticed is that poor speeches have two things in common: they are disorganized and they go on for way too long. From what I can tell, it sounds as though the student writes out a finished product from the very beginning. As a result, there's a tendency for the topic to meander along with no real plan. A speech will start on the variety of shoes available to customers and move into the importance of walking and finish with an urge toward buying a good pair of socks. In addition, since there is no real plan, there's no real way to know what the point is, or when we're ever going to get there. Clearly, this places a premium on editing.

Editing Means Adding More $!#&*@, Right?

So, you have before you a speech with no real direction and you're told that you need to edit it. The problem with that directive is that most people assume that you need to add more. So, you take a bad speech and you make it worse by making it longer. That is not a recipe for a great speech.

Find the Problem and Purpose

Before writing out a speech, take a moment to determine a problem and a purpose.

For an informative speech, think about what needs audiences might have. In other words, what's missing in their lives? What could you show them that would help to make their lives better?

For a persuasive speech, think about what people are doing, thinking, or believing (or not doing, not thinking, or not believing). What should they be doing, thinking, or believing instead? What's it going to take to convince them to change?

With that, let's look at a very simple method of organizing your speech for maximum effectiveness.

Try the OABD Method

Outline   Make a broad outline that includes the topic (i.e. the problem) and the purpose. List the main points or arguments of the discussion.

Add   Under each main point or argument, add your support. This will include assertions (claims), explanations, and examples. Bring in some numbers (i.e. statistics), and some quotes from qualified individuals.

Back-up For every claim (every fact and figure), find a credible source that backs it up. Note it right next to each statement making the claim or revealing the numbers.

Delete Now that you have everything arranged, take out anything that is not dedicated to addressing the topic/problem or furthers the purpose of the speech.

This method will allow you to piece together a speech that includes only ideas dedicated toward fulfilling the purpose of your speech. Anything else is a waste of your time and the audience's time.

By outlining, you have a simple framework that allows you to see where you want to go. Adding things gives you a chance to put all of your ideas and research onto paper. Backing up what you say with sources gives you the credibility needed in a speech. Deleting then helps you to keep it short and powerful. Less is more in this case. Edit for effectiveness.

CHAPTER 4

TYPES OF SPEECHES

INFORMATIVE SPEECHES—TEACHING TO THE CHOIR

If you want your speech to be a good one, then you need to give it some purpose. Of course, what is that purpose? If you find yourself saying to yourself that you really just want to get the speech over with, then that's your purpose. Do you think the audience will be thrilled about that?

The key word here is "relevance." Almost any topic you choose can be a good one as long as you make it relevant to the audience. That's the real trick. Some of that was covered in "Crafting an Introduction" and "The Importance of the Introduction," but let's look at it more carefully as it pertains to informative speeches.

So, with that in mind, the purpose of any informative, or persuasiv, speech is to identify a problem and provide a solution. (In persuasive speeches, you have to go the extra step of proving the problem really exists.) But, if the audience already agrees that the problem exists, then you don't need to spend a lot of time preaching to the choir. You need to focus on teaching the choir—hopefully not how to sing!

To make this a bit easier, I have developed a "fill in the blank" system to help you begin the process of developing your topic/purpose/relevance. This will help you to frame the problem, identify the cause, and determine the solution.

For informative speeches, there is an accepted lack of understanding or a missing skill set among the audience members. The "problem" in the audience is that they need this understanding or skill set in order to be successful at something. As a speaker, you must identify this problem, the missing knowledge or skill, and outline how this knowledge or skill will enhance the lives of the audience members. You can begin by completing the outline and directions below:

1. People don't know how to _____.

How many people don't know? List your source.

You need some evidence that this is truly a problem within the audience or within society and you need a credible source that indicates that.

2. This is a problem because _____.

Provide an example or statistic. List your source.

Again, a missing skill set is only a problem if it hinders the audience's lives somehow. We may not know how to ice skate or knit a sweater, but if we've gotten along just fine without those skills, then how is it relevant to us? This is why you have to address this. Without it, you are just providing useless information. People won't know or care about economics until you determine that economics has an impact on them (particularly, their money).

3. If it doesn't change, _____ **could be the result. But, if it does change,** _____ **could be the result.**

Provide some evidence this could be true. List your source.

So, to use the economics example, if people don't understand the principles of the economy, what could be the result? Can unaware individuals potentially lose a lot of money? Can they find themselves with less purchasing power? Working harder and earning less? If so, what examples can you provide to show us this is possible?

Of course, the next steps involve developing that understanding or missing skill set for us, but the important thing here is to frame the problem in a way that has a potential impact upon the audience. Once the audience can see how the problem relates to the missing skill, they will be eager to listen to you in order to correct the problem. The more you develop this aspect of your speech or presentation, the more willing your audience will be to listen.

Remember, the audience is aware that they are missing some things in their lives. They just don't see how those things always matter to them. Once they see the link, they will want to get the know-how to improve their lot. And, yes, if the choir can't sing, then they will want to learn!

INFORMATIVE SPEECH TEMPLATE

Just in case all of this great advice becomes a bit overwhelming, I have for you a basic template for developing a speech. Follow the steps, answer the questions (after much thought and research), put it all together, and smooth it all out. You'll have yourself speech that went from pretty good to even better!

Choosing a Topic/Purpose

Key word: *Relevance*—the purpose of any informative or persuasive speech is to identify the problem and provide the solution. Determine a problem, cause, and solution.

Informative speeches: lack of understanding, missing skill set

There's a problem that requires you to obtain specific knowledge or skill. Identify the missing knowledge or skill set. Outline how the knowledge or skill set will enhance our lives.

Basic types:

- How to do something: Investing in the stock market
- How something works: Cultivation theory of media

Types of Speeches

1. People don't know how to _____.

How many people don't know?

_____
_____
_____
_____

List your source. _____

2. This is a problem because _____.

Provide an example or statistic.

_____
_____
_____
_____

List your source. _____

3. If it doesn't change, _____ **could be the result.**

Provide evidence this is true.

_____
_____
_____
_____

List your source. _____

Introduction

1. Attention-getter

Give us a sense that there may be something wrong or missing in our lives with a...

- hypothetical question
- imagined scenario
- shocking statistic (and source) or shocking statement/assertion
- very brief story/anecdote/joke (related to the topic)

_____
_____
_____
_____
_____

List your source. _____

2. Lead into the problem (the topic of discussion)

So, what's this all about? You got our interest, now what's the problem? How does it affect us?

_____
_____
_____
_____
_____

3. Show us the problem is real with...

- Statistics—show us how with some numbers (add source)
- A quote from a trusted authority

Types of Speeches

_____
_____
_____
_____
_____
_____

List your source. _____
_____

4. Assure us that there is a "solution"

Now that you've shown us we have a potential or real problem on our hands, help us learn how to fix it or change it.

_____
_____
_____
_____

5. Provide us with a "quick list" of 2-5 main points of discussion

Make sure they are short phrases that can be listed.

> *Example: When considering the prospect of building your own computer, the four main parts to consider are: the motherboard, processor, memory, and storage space.*

Informative: Provide us with the basic elements of how to do something:
- step by step directions
- list of functions or items
- considerations before engaging

Main points to consider include:
1. _____
2. _____
3. _____
4. _____
5. _____

_____
_____
_____
_____

_____
_____

Body

1. Transition from Introduction to Main Point #1

"First, let's look at (Main Point #1)…"

Example (how to do something): "Let's examine the first step: assessing the target."

Example (how something works): "The first principle of cultivation is that increased exposure to media materials creates (or cultivates) a world view consistent with what is seen (on television)."

_____
_____
_____
_____
_____

2. Main Point #1

- Explanation of the step/idea/argument
- Clarify with an example/statistic/testimony
- Add quote from trusted source or testimonial (optional)
- What are we to make of this point?

_____
_____
_____

Types of Speeches

List your source. _____

3. Transition from Main Point #1 to Main Point #2
- "Next, let's examine (Main Point #2)..."
- "Now that we've looked at Main Point #1, let's move on to Main Point #2..."

Example (transition from previous point to next point—benefit of changing): "We've looked at some of the consequences of not taking charge of your financial situation, but now let's look at what we can do to avoid problems with money. By adopting this simple budget plan, you can save $3,000 within the first year."

4. Main Point #2 (Make sure it's about the same length of time as Main Point #1)
- Explanation of the step/idea/argument
- How is it different than Main Point #1?
- Clarify with an example/statistic/testimony
- Add quote from trusted source or testimonial (optional)
- What are we to make of this point?

List your source. _____
_____

5. Transition from Main Point #2 to Main Point #3

- Finally (if this is the last point), let's examine (Main Point #3)…
- Now that we've looked at Main Point #2, let's move on to Main Point #3…

_____
_____
_____
_____
_____

6. Main Point #3 (Make sure it's about the same length as Main Point #2)

- Explanation of the step/idea/argument
- How is it different than Main Point #1 and Main Point #2?
- Clarify with an example/statistic/testimony
- Add quote from trusted source or testimonial (optional)
- What are we to make of this point?

   Example (account for counter-argument): "Now, you might be thinking, 'Yeah, but budgets mean less spending and less fun.' While this plan may require that you spend less money, it doesn't mean you can't enjoy the activities you have in the past."

_____
_____
_____
_____
_____

List your source. _____
_____

Conclusion

1. Transition into Conclusion

"In conclusion…" It's okay—not great, but okay. Pause. Wait a second or two, and then move into…

2. Review the original problem

_____
_____
_____
_____
_____

3. Review the main points

_____
_____
_____
_____
_____

4. Show us how the main points solve the problem

_____
_____
_____
_____
_____

5. What do we do next?

Tell us what we can do next

_____
_____
_____

6. Give us some encouragement that we will be better off in the future.

7. Say "thank you."

8. Enjoy the applause

PERSUASIVE SPEECHES: ASSESSING THE NEED FOR CHANGE

Persuasion is change. It is not simply providing a list of pros and cons and leaving the decision up to the audience. It is not a litany of opinions on how the world ought to be. It is not even a series of facts about a product with a suggestion that the audience "ought to buy sometime soon... maybe... in the future... if you want to...."

In their most basic form, persuasive speeches identify a need for change, provide arguments for change, outline a plan that will facilitate change, and urge us to action. Of course, that's easier said than done, as evidenced by the descriptions above of what a persuasive speech is not. So, let's look more closely at these basic elements to develop more powerful persuasive speeches.

Understanding Persuasion

As stated boldly in the beginning, persuasion is change. If you walk into a room full of people who love ice cream and say, "I'm here to convince you that ice cream is a wonderful thing," you really don't have a lot of work to do. If everyone already agrees with you, then you haven't changed them in any way. You might have whipped up a frenzy, and maybe everyone is ready to go get some ice cream, but their attitude toward ice cream was unchanged.

So, before persuasion can even begin, you have to assess a need for change.

Assessing Need for Change

Now that you know that change is a necessary condition for persuasion, you can begin the process of assessing the need for change. There's a fairly simple way to do that, though it will require some work on your part. First, determine what your goal is by filling in the blank:

The Ideal

I want people to do/think/believe _____.

Keeping with the ice cream example, let's say you are thinking about trying to convince people that ice cream is a good thing. But before you can even do that, you have to fill in the blank:

The Current Condition

People are doing/thinking/believing _____.

What sources/evidence supports your claim?

So, are people not eating ice cream? Do they think it's wrong to eat it? Do they believe the hype against ice cream?

Notice the question of sources and evidence to support your claim that people are acting or thinking in a certain way. It's one thing to fill in the blank and make such a declaration, but is it true? How do we know you are not making some wild claim?

It's easy enough to say "millions of people across America are not eating ice cream despite it being the most delicious treat ever!" But, how many millions of people are behaving this way? Where did you pull that (rather vague) number? Is that information reliable?

If your response is that we ought to just trust you because you know it's true, then you can be sure that your premise (i.e. the condition) is a faulty one, circumstantial at best. In short, we need some evidence that supports your belief in the condition before you can move them toward changing to the ideal.

Arguments and Counter-Arguments

Arguments are often confused with features. For example, claiming that "there's tons of different flavors available" may or may not be true (again, where's the evidence?) but more importantly, how exactly does that convince an audience they want to eat ice cream? What you really need is to assess three simple ideas:

Consequences

> *If people don't do/think/believe the ideal (see above),*
> *_____ will be the result (generally bad).*

Again, provide evidence and sources that support this possibility.

Benefits

> *If people do/think/believe the ideal, _____ will result (generally good).*

Again and always, provide evidence and sources that support this possibility.

Resistance

> *People may not wish to do/think/believe in the ideal*
> *because _____, but that's not a valid reason because*
> *_____.*

For both, bring the evidence and the sources.

This will be perhaps the most time-consuming portion of your speech, and it certainly will require a lot of research, but that is a necessary function of change. Audiences are not going to believe you just because you say so. Evidence and reason (making sense of the evidence) will ultimately bring about change.

Plan

Often overlooked in persuasive speeches, providing a plan of action may be little more than simply encouraging the audience to believe what you want them to believe (i.e. the ideal) rather than what they already believe (the current condition). However, some topics may leave the audience ready for change, but with no real idea of how to change. Even though this becomes almost an informative speech at this point, bringing in an outline for change will often help facilitate that change.

For example, let's say you are trying to convince an audience of smokers to stop smoking. You've gotten all the research you need to show them consequences of continuing to smoke, evidence of the benefits for quitting, and you've even addressed the reasons they might resist quitting. They are ready to quit, but they don't have a plan. Left without a plan, they might easily shrug and continue to smoke. Giving them a plan (the nicotine candy bar plan, the cold turkey sandwich plan) will help them feel like there's a way to change.

Urge to Action

Finally, you must spend a little time urging the audience to act (change). This is probably best done as part of your conclusion. Spend some time summarizing the major arguments (consequences, benefits, resistance) to help them see how the ideal is far better than the current condition. Ask or demand that they change, and ask or demand that they change immediately. Don't be afraid to add in the sense of urgency. Add in the emotion. Perhaps you can bring in anecdotal evidence as a final argument; maybe you changed a long time ago and you are now enjoying a better quality of life than before.

Remember, change is the purpose of this speech. Understanding that is the key to success. Develop that need for change by determining where your audience is and where you want them to go. Show them the need for change with the benefits of changing and the consequences for not changing. Assure them that there's a plan available to them, and spend some time urging them to act. Make sure you bring in the research that backs you up, and you will have a powerful persuasive speech.

PERSUASIVE SPEECH TEMPLATE

You might notice this template is very nearly the same as the informative speech. In terms of formatting, it is the same. The only difference might be that the main points will typically include arguments that help to change beliefs or feelings or actions.

Choosing a Topic/Purpose

Key word: *Relevance*—the purpose of any informative or persuasive speech is to identify the problem and provide the solution. Determine a problem, cause, and solution.

Persuasive speeches: change is necessary for success/survival

There's a problem that requires you to change what you think/do.

Basic Types:
- Believe these facts: The moon landing never took place.
- Adopt these values: Stem cell research can be helpful/harmful.
- Adopt this policy: Stop smoking now.

Types of Speeches

1. People are doing/thinking/believing _____.

How many people do/think/believe that?

_____
_____
_____
_____
_____

List your source. _____
_____

2. Instead, they need to do/think/believe _____.

Provide an example or statistic.

_____
_____
_____
_____
_____

List your source. _____
_____

3. If they don't change, _____ **could be the result.**

Provide evidence this is true.

_____
_____
_____
_____
_____

List your source. _____
_____

Introduction

1. Attention-getter

Give us a sense that there may be something wrong or missing in our lives with a...

- hypothetical question
- imagined scenario
- shocking statistic (and source) or shocking statement/assertion
- very brief story/anecdote/joke (related to the topic)

2. Lead into the problem (the topic of discussion)

So, what's this all about? You got our interest, now what's the problem? How does it affect us?

3. Show us the problem is real with...

- Statistics (show us how with some numbers). Add source.
- A quote from a trusted authority

4. Assure us that there is a "solution"

Now that you've shown us we have a potential or real problem on our hands, help us think/act/believe differently.

5. Provide us with a "quick list" of 2-5 main points of discussion
- Make sure they are short phrases that can be listed.
- Provide us with the arguments that will persuade us to change and the solution.

1. Arguments
   - Consequences of not changing
   - Benefits for changing

List your source: _____

2. Account for counter-arguments
   - Why our reasons for resistance are invalid

List your source: _____

3. Game plan for change (How to actually do it)

List your source: _____

Body

1. Transition from Introduction to Main Point #1

Example (argument—consequence of not changing): "First, smoking reduces lung capacity."

2. Main Point #1

- Explanation of the step/idea/argument
- Clarify with an example/statistic/testimony
- Add quote from trusted source or testimonial (optional)
- What are we to make of this point?

Types of Speeches

_____
_____
_____
_____
_____

List your source: _____

3. Transition from Main Point #1 to Main Point #2
- "Next, let's examine (Main Point #2)…"
- "Now that we've looked at Main Point #1, let's move on to Main Point #2…"

   Example (transition from previous point to next point—benefit of changing): "We've looked at some of the consequences of not taking charge of your financial situation, but now let's look at what we can do to avoid problems with money. By adopting this simple budget plan, you can save $3,000 within the first year."

_____
_____
_____
_____
_____

List your source: _____

4. Main Point #2 (Make sure it's about the same length of time as Main Point #1)
- Explanation of the step/idea/argument
- How is it different than Main Point #1?
- Clarify with an example/statistic/testimony
- Add quote from trusted source or testimonial (optional)
- What are we to make of this point?

5. Transition from Main Point #2 to Main Point #3
- Finally (if this is the last point), let's examine (Main Point #3)…
- Now that we've looked at Main Point #2, let's move on to Main Point #3…

List your source: _____

6. Main Point #3 (Make sure it's about the same length as Main Point #2)
- Explanation of the step/idea/argument
- How is it different than Main Point #1 and Main Point #2?
- Clarify with an example/statistic/testimony
- Add quote from trusted source or testimonial (optional)
- What are we to make of this point?

Example (account for counter-argument): "Now, you might be thinking, "Yeah, but budgets mean less spending and less fun." While this plan may require that you spend less money, it doesn't mean you can't enjoy the activities you have in the past."

List your source: _____

Conclusion

1. Transition into Conclusion.
- "In conclusion…"
- It's okay—not great, but okay.
- Pause
- Wait a second or two, and then move into…

2. Review the original problem.

3. Review the main points.

4. Show us how the main points solve the problem.

5. What do we do next?

- Urge us to action

List your source: _____

6. Give us some encouragement that we will be better off in the future.

7. Say, "Thank you."

8. Enjoy the applause.

COMMEMORATIVE SPEECHES: NEVER SAY 'ALWAYS'

Commemorative speeches come from the heart, so it feels unnatural to force it into a format. Unfortunately, without a format, there's chaos, or what I call a "really, really bad speech." What does this speech sound like? More importantly, how can we develop a commemorative speech that will honor the individual or group while inspiring the audience?

Never Say "Never" or "Always"

When you are asked to talk about someone in glowing terms, the task seems a bit daunting. How do you express how much this person means to you or to the audience? How do you make this person seem special?

The answer usually comes in the form of meaningless platitudes strung together with awkward pauses and nervous smiles. The empty compliments somehow are designed to show real emotion. To prove this, superlatives like "always" and "never" appear, giving the individual saint-like qualities.

But, as I said, they are empty. Let me show you why. Let's first commemorate Uncle Bob, then switch it up to Cousin Kari. Read each speech, and notice something very strange (and a little sad).

Let's start with Uncle Bob:

> "Uncle Bob is a great guy. What can I say? He's always there for me. He's the kind of guy that would give the shirt off of his back for you. We're always laughing and joking and stuff. He's got a really big heart; he's always doing things to help people. He never has a bad thing to say about anyone, and in conclusion, I think Uncle Bob is the most loving, most generous person I know."

Sorry if that doesn't bring tears to my eyes. Let's now commemorate Cousin Kari and see why this speech just falls flat:

> "Cousin Kari is a great lady. What can I say? She's always there for me. She's the kind of person that would give the shirt off of her back for you. We're always laughing and joking and

stuff. She's got a really big heart; she's always doing things to help people. She never has a bad thing to say about anyone, and in conclusion, I think Cousin Kari is the most loving, most generous person I know."

Uh… that was nearly identical. And, that's what I'm talking about. These speeches are virtually meaningless because they can apply to almost anyone. Just take out "Uncle Bob" or "Cousin Kari" and add anyone's name, and you have a speech that is about as uninspiring as they come. Adding "always" and "never" doesn't make it any better. In fact, if someone is always laughing, they are probably insane.

So, what can we do?

Qualities and Memories

Rather than worry about formatting, take a moment to think about what exactly you admire in other people. That will vary from person to person or group to group, but ultimately, the things you admire about people are qualities that define their character.

So, in this example, Uncle Bob or Cousin Kari seem to be loyal ("always there for me"), giving, fun, loving, generous, and kind. That's quite a few qualities, and you probably only need to focus on one or two.

But, for each of these qualities, think of a memory of that person that you share with them that exemplifies that quality. Don't spread it thin by claiming they are "always" doing generous things. Think of a time that this person showed true generosity. What happened exactly? Why was this moment or memory so important to you (why do you remember it so clearly)?

A Moment in Time

You see, we aren't inspired by people who are able to "always" do things. We are inspired by the quality of their character, especially when we can see it in action. So, rather than claim that someone is good, show us that goodness in his or her actions. Paint a picture. Take us back to that moment in time:

> *"Uncle Bob may not have been perfect, but he was very generous to those he loved. I think of the time when I was in eighth grade, and I wanted to make the basketball team more than anything. The problem was, I didn't really know the fundamentals, so my chances were looking slim. But, Uncle Bob, who was quite the star in high school, spent the entire summer working with me. He showed me how to dribble and shoot and pass. By the time tryouts came, I felt ready. I made the team thanks to Uncle Bob, who was so generous with his time."*

Okay, maybe tears aren't flowing here, either, but at least we have a real memory tied to a quality. Instead of Uncle Bob being the "most generous" person on the planet (how does one even get that distinction?), we get to see uncle Bob doing something generous: giving his time to teach you how to play basketball is a very generous act. No, he won't win the Nobel Prize, but he made a difference in your life, and that is meaningful.

Make It Meaningful

For a commemorative speech, that's all it really comes down to: making it meaningful. The format isn't such a big deal. If you took the example above and only used that as your entire speech, you'd be better off than someone who strings together the platitudes for a few agonizing minutes.

Of course, to make it meaningful, you need to spell out what that quality signifies. In other words, why are you discussing this? Why are you commemorating Uncle Bob? Why did you choose that quality? How does it fit within the context of the occasion?

> *"I wanted to thank Uncle Bob for being so generous with his time. It made a big difference in my life at a time when I needed it most. It's a debt I can't directly repay, but a lesson I can take with me and instill in others. That's why we are dedicating this gymnasium to my uncle..."*

You get the idea. Now, we know that this story of generosity has led to the dedication of a building that will help other kids learn to play basketball. That tugs at the heart strings a little more.

Remember, it's not a competition to see how many good or great qualities you can list. It's not about turning someone into a saint. It's about celebrating that individual or group on a personal level by sharing what you admire about them and the specific memories you have that exemplify the qualities you admire. That comes from the heart, and will inspire others... always.

COMMEMORATIVE SPEECH TEMPLATE
Introduction

Who are you commemorating? Briefly discuss the background of the person, group, or institution. You can tell us a little about where they came from, what they did or do in life (you don't have to wait until someone passes to give an inspiring speech about that person!). Then, hint that this person (or group or institution) is more than just the things they did or accomplished. Mention that they have qualities that make them special.

What qualities do you admire? (Three is usually good, but you can go up to five if you wish.)

1. _____
2. _____
3. _____
4. _____
5. _____

Body

At this point, describe the quality you admire by giving a story that took place in time. As mentioned, don't fall back on vague memories that seem to involve the words "always" or "never." Be very specific.

Quality #1 (Main Point #1)
Tell us a story that illustrates this quality ("This one time....")

List your source: _____

Quality #2 (Main Point #2)
Tell us a story that illustrates this quality ("This one time....")

List your source: _____

Quality #3 (Main Point #3)
Tell us a story that illustrates this quality ("This one time....")

List your source: _____

Quality #4 (Main Point #4)
Tell us a story that illustrates this quality ("This one time....")

_____
_____
_____
_____
_____

List your source: _____

Quality #5 (Main Point #5)
Tell us a story that illustrates this quality ("This one time....")

_____
_____
_____
_____
_____

List your source: _____

Conclusion

Tell us how much this person is loved, how much you admire them and why, and what their life and qualities (his or her character) mean to you or us.

_____
_____
_____
_____
_____

AFTER DINNER SPEECH: NO LAUGHTER REQUIRED

I've given three best-man speeches at weddings, and the one thing I've always noticed is that the audience is a little antsy. They want to eat, and the last thing they want to hear is the best man and the maid of honor prattle on about how great "Jessica and Todd" are together and how their love will conquer all and other over the top sugar-filled statements. I often thought that the speech would be far better received if it could be given… after dinner.

> Of course, this leads into the basic question: what is an after-dinner speech?
>
> That question is usually followed by, "Is it, like, jokes or a funny story or something like that?"
>
> Yeah, something like that.

Focus on Fun

After-dinner speeches are tougher to nail down because they can be just about anything as long as it is fun. Audiences should come away from the experience with a smile on their face. Any laughs you can provide are icing on the cake.

To that end, we must recognize the most important rule of an after-dinner speech: Do not bum the audience out.

This is not the time to talk about puppies getting hurt or relatives suffering from financial woes. Don't mention anyone dying. I know it seems intuitive, but some speakers forget that the occasion is meant to be a happy one, and as a speaker, your job is to keep the good feelings going. Talk about almost anything else, as long as it is fun. The focus is on fun. Fun. Not sad. Fun.

But, because the only purpose of this speech is for the audience to enjoy the experience of the speech or the occasion, this means that identifying a problem and a solution (the foundation of informative or persuasive speeches) don't really apply, and as a result, you might feel a little lost. So, what do you do?

After-Dinner Considerations

The only way to know what to do is to understand what not to do. After-dinner speeches can come in many forms, but here are a few things to keep in mind:

Format the introduction I'm not suggesting you have to have a preview of main points ("I'll tell you about the camping trip from hell by looking at the nightmares of packing, the nonstop rain, and the flat tire on the way home") even though that would work just fine. At least we know what the highlights will be. But, we need some idea of what to expect. An introduction into the story or topic helps give us the structure we crave.

No stand-up routines After-dinner speeches still require the same rigorous development as any other speech. You can't just get up there and start telling knock-knock jokes or ask, "What's the deal with airline peanuts?" If you find yourself doing that trick where it looks like you're detaching your thumb, you've sunk to a new low. If I see you doing that, I'll be laughing, but for entirely different reasons.

No random stories Again, the point here is that you need some formatting: introduction, body, and conclusion. Don't just say something like, "Okay, I'm going to tell you a story, okay? Ready? Go." The problem is that this is followed by a rambling story that we have no idea when it will end. If the story is amusing, you can spend a moment setting it up.

Research within Since many topics often deal with more personal matters, research might not necessarily be formal in the sense that you search through documents or gather statistics, but it will require experiences that can be described in an amusing manner. Think about your story or topic and see if you can find a fun way to tell the story.

Laughter not required "I'm just not funny!" I hear that all the time, and it's not true. Anyone can be amusing. Just loosen up a bit. Relax. Laugh a little at yourself. Be a little silly and like it. But, remember that an after-dinner speech doesn't need to be funny. It just needs to be fun. So, if you find that you can't get people slapping their knees with your clever word play or goofy sounds, go for heart-warming. Smiles work just as well.

Appropriate topics As I said, anything that bums out the audience is bad. Embarrassing stories seem like a way to get a quick laugh, but if you aren't the topic, this is dangerous ground. People get upset when they feel like they look stupid or silly. The best way to decide if the topic is okay is to imagine the youngest or most conservative person in the audience. If you feel uncomfortable discussing it in front of them, then change the topic.

What Can I Say?

But, what topics can you discuss? What kind of speech would work? Well, that depends on the venue. For example, a wedding will probably include speeches about the couple. All you have to do is not say anything that might upset the couple or the crowd (i.e. past relationships, individual shortcomings of the couple, or bets on how long the marriage will last). For other occasions, this might not be as obvious. You might be asked to simply get up and entertain the extended family at a reunion. Now what? Well, again, the venue often decides the topic.

Just find a way to relate to the audience and discuss the matter in a way that makes it fun: not-so-miserable camping trips, growing pains between mother and daughter, grocery store trip that took five hours, why Uncle Bob is the coolest and craziest guy ever, and so on.

Where's the Roast Beef?

Most after-dinner speeches won't actually involve a meal. I often wish they would. When people eat food, there's generally a better overall mood felt by the crowd. That makes it easier to engage the audience. Just remember that when you do, keep the good mood going by developing a speech that will at least put a smile on their face. The audience will forget the words, but they won't forget the feeling.

After Dinner Speech Template

There's no exact formula to develop this speech, but I'll provide one here for you. It might help. It might change—in the next edition!

Think of an event that occurred related to a particular topic. It may or may not have been fun or funny at the time, but maybe now you can look back on it and laugh. If you can't, then maybe others can, depending on how you tell the story.

For your introduction, I'll let you determine how much of the format you want to follow, but somewhere in there, you ought to mention the main points (i.e. the preview of main points). For this particular template, the main points would be: "what happened and what I learned," or you could list some of the major events and then make another point about lessons learned.

What happened?

_____
_____
_____
_____
_____
_____
_____
_____

What was learned from the experience (something ironic or patently obvious in retrospect)?

In conclusion, what advice would you give to others regarding this? Remember to keep it fun.

TWO-POINT BUSINESS PRESENTATION

Going from a speech class to the company boardroom, there seems to be a bit of a disconnect. How can the format of the Pretty Good Speech apply to a business proposal or presentation? It seems like you only have a few minutes to discuss the situation, and most people in the meeting already know the context, so it makes the introduction (with the attention-getter, lead into the topic, etc.) an awkward step in the process. In fact, why can't business presentations just get right to the point?

I can't argue with that.

So, how about we develop a new format that gets right to the point? This speech will get right to the good stuff, providing only two points: the problem and the solution. We'll call it the Two-Point (Business) Presentation.

Attention-Getter: The Problem

By definition, the first thing you say or do is your attention-getter. However, instead of asking a rhetorical question or (God forbid) busting a Webster's dictionary definition, get the group's attention by not mincing words: state the problem.

> *"Let's get to the point: our company is losing money– $10 billion last quarter to be exact, according to our accountants."*

Notice that a source was still used (this one just happens to be in-house, but it's still a credible source... I hope). And, believe me, if you lost $10 billion, you'll have their attention!

The Problem (Context, Development, and Consequences)

Now that you've got their attention, contextualize the problem. That is, take a moment to show what's going on inside or outside of the company that may have led to this problem. What are the media saying (quote them and cite the sources)?

Then, spend a moment developing the problem. In other words, provide a brief overview of how the problem came into existence. In the example above, discuss how the company lost $10 billion and how other companies in the industry are doing.

Finally, suggest the consequences of not doing something. If things go unchanged, what will be the result? Provide a source or quote or some evidence this is a real possibility, such as a cautionary example ("Company X had the same situation last year and had to file for bankruptcy protection.") Finish that by stating that something has to change. This will be a good segue into the next main point....

The Solution (How It Works and How It Benefits Us)

Now that the group understands how serious the situation is and how it can spiral out of control, bring in the proposed solution. Show the group how the solution would work (outline the plan) and discuss the benefits of adopting the solution.

Close the Deal

Since this is a business presentation, there's no need to say "In conclusion..." or try to find some clever way to weave all of the main points into some kind of summary. What you need to do is close the deal. Since this is a proposed solution, you need to really sell it somehow. It's a little beyond the scope of this article to provide closing techniques. But, essentially, you need to ask or demand that your idea gets adopted.

> *"Ladies and gentleman, we know the problem is big, and we know that it can get bigger if we don't act now. My plan is to reduce costs and boost sales by up to 35% over the next three months. The only question is: are you willing to accept this plan?"*

Notice that there is still a brief summary provided. This allows the group to completely digest what has been said and what needs to be done. In this example, a question is posed. You could just as easily make a statement like:

> *"Let's get started!"*

Again, this urge to action may not be much, but it might be the difference between getting the deal or not. It's certainly a stronger conclusion than saying, "Maybe—I don't know—it seems like it could work, so..." Be sure to shrug your shoulders to guarantee that no one will be impressed.

What about the Format?

As I often claim, the format that I've taught over the years isn't necessarily the best way to go about developing a speech; it's a good way (hence, the whole "pretty good" thing we have going on here). So, all of the best speeches will not follow the format. But, all of the worst speeches (and I'm sure you've heard your share and maybe even contributed your share) also don't follow the format. We've aimed for somewhere in the middle.

In business, and quite possibly in all areas, time is of the essence. The format we've used previously is a good way to develop your thinking. Once you've mastered it, you can find more efficient ways to solve the problem of public speaking (of communicating). Getting to the point very rarely upsets people who value time. Understanding this, you can learn to bend the rules a bit. In the end, it's about the audience, so if they want just the facts, then give them just the facts.

TWO-POINT BUSINESS PRESENTATION TEMPLATE

You don't have to follow this to the letter, but here's a nice template to help you organize your work.

Introduction

Here's the problem:

_____
_____
_____
_____

List your source: _____

Main Point #1: How the problem developed

Company history of the problem:

_____
_____
_____
_____

List your source: _____

Others in the industry that suffered the problem:
_____
_____
_____
_____
_____

The possible consequences of not dealing with the problem:
_____
_____
_____
_____
_____

List your source: _____

Main Point #2: The solution

Explanation of the solution:
_____
_____
_____
_____
_____

List your source: _____

Benefits and evidence of the solution working:
_____
_____
_____

List your source: _____

Reasons why this solution is better than others proposed:

List your source: _____

Possible counter arguments and why they aren't valid:

List your source: _____

Conclusion: Urge to action

Restate the problem:

Restate the consequences of not dealing with it:

_____
_____
_____
_____

Restate the proposition of your solution:

_____
_____
_____
_____

Assure the audience of the soundness of approving the proposition:

_____
_____
_____
_____

List your source: _____
_____

IMPROMPTU SPEECH

It's the nightmare of public speaking nightmares; you find out that you will be expected to discuss some topic in the next ten minutes during a meeting, conference call, or banquet hall event. Had you a week or a day or at least an hour, you could have had something good prepared. But now it looks like you'll be fumbling your way through something and looking and feeling as stupid as one could possibly feel. Oh, those dreadful impromptu speeches!

Fear not, friends! There's a way to get through it.

Ground Rules

First, there are few things that have to happen prior to developing an impromptu speech. First, and from now on, you have to be in a cat-like state of readiness. In other words, you have to always be ready to say a few words on a given topic.

In most cases, you'll have some working knowledge of the issue. If you are walking into a meeting regarding a project you have been working on, you should have some level of detail at your command. If you are at a party and someone asks you to introduce the guest of honor or say a few things about her, you should be able to do this, unless you have no idea who this person is. And, that would be strange, since most people attending would know the honored guest, and certainly no one would ask you to speak unless you knew that person. But, I guess stranger things have happened.

Knowing that at any moment you could be asked to speak, you need to be caught up with just about everything. Watch the news. Pay attention in staff meetings. Take notes. Ask questions. Look up sources of information. Find out the latest trends. Watch a few movies and a few popular television programs. Listen to some music. Read some good books and magazines. Be engaged with the world around you. As I always say: do your research.

Having a broad-based knowledge of current and historic events, popular and high culture, literature, science, and arts will make you a more well-rounded individual, but will also allow you to discuss a wide range of topics or to add to a particular topic. You'll be able to bring in different perspectives to a given topic.

Formatting the Chaos

With these ground rules in place, we now concentrate on the basics. I have always urged readers to follow a basic format. But, when you are pressed to discuss things with little to no time for preparation, you have to cut a few corners and make the most of what time you do have. So, let's say you have exactly two minutes to prepare a speech. For the sake of this exercise, we'll assume that you are asked to give an informative speech regarding some topic.

1. Quickly jot down a list of 2-3 points the audience absolutely needs to know. These will be your MAIN POINTS. (PREVIEW)
2. Answer this question: Why do they need to know this? (PURPOSE)
3. How big is this issue? If you have numbers and a source you can quote, then jot those down. (CREDIBILITY/RELATING TO AUDIENCE)
4. Write down a question related to the topic that could pique the interest of the audience. (ATTENTION-GETTER)

Rearrange the Order and Run

You've just worked the introduction out backwards, so all you need to do is turn it all around and go from there. If you find that you have time for only the first three, then you can use your credibility statement as an attention-getter.

So, start with your attention-getter. Add in your credibility statement, which will give the audience a sense of the urgency of the message or perhaps some sense of how this topic impacts many others. The fact that you can quote some source (thanks to all your research) will prove to be quite impressive. Next, state the purpose or goal of your speech or discussion, then list the points you plan to discuss (i.e. the preview of the main points).

From there, you transition into each of the points with comments like "First," "Second," "Next," and "Finally." Or, you can be even more clever, and transition from point to point by saying, "We've looked at [MAIN POINT #1], but now let's focus on [MAIN POINT #2]." Or, you can transition by asking a question.

You'll notice that the body of the speech will be where you spend most of your time "riffing" (i.e. fumbling for the right words). But, if you have the main points in place, and you have a good working knowledge of these points, you should not have too many problems discussing them in some detail. If you don't, then (as I always say) you need to do your research.

A Format by Any Other Name

For those of you who are asked to discuss a business issue, you can always master the art and development of the two-point business presentation, but these are essentially the same thing. The idea is that you have to quickly relate to the audience the problem, the purpose, and the points (information or the arguments) that will ultimately lead to some solution or resolution. The format is the thing.

Good, Not Great—Good Enough

Once you know how to format the speech– particularly the introduction– you have all the pieces of the puzzle you need to quickly develop a speech. Of course, this speech will not be as good as the one you can take time to develop. In fact, this format can often lead to speeches that sound a bit mechanical: "Do you like eggs? Well, lots of people do, but they don't know how to pick the right egg. I will show you how to do that by looking at the size, texture, and price."

It's all there. It's not exactly the greatest introduction (or topic) ever created, but it does what we need it to do. And, given the amount of time you have to develop such a speech, I think it'll do much better than saying, "Uh, I guess I'll talk about eggs for awhile, okay? Um, what is an egg? What can we do about them? Um, I don't know. Let's see. They have yolks." And on and on… painfully on and on for you and the audience.

I know which speech I'd rather hear. Which one would you rather give?

CHAPTER 5

RESEARCH—KNOW YOUR STUFF

GATHERING GOOD INFORMATION

If you remember nothing else from this chapter, please remember this: have a healthy dose of skepticism when reviewing information. I know that preparing reports or presentations can be quite time-consuming and arduous. It's tough enough to face the prospect of delivering a presentation; you certainly don't need the hassle of fact-checking... or do you?

Absolutely, yes, you do. Why? Quite simply, just about anyone can put just about anything on the web. Truth is optional. Facts become matters of opinion. Research, then, is a question of who gets cited first on a Google™ search.

Remember that any time you make any assertion that remotely sounds like a fact, you need documentation that backs it up. What are things that sound like facts? That's not the easiest question to answer, but I'll say that anything that has a date (year) or quantity (number) or speaks to an event that has taken place or is taking place. Also, anything that is quoted or paraphrased has to have a source.

That being said, some sources are better than others. So, please, take a moment to consider the following when developing your research.

Who is the source?

This is an important question to ask because it leads into more important questions, specifically: what are the qualifications of the source?

If you're getting your information from a blog, how trustworthy is the source? And, yes, go ahead and ask that person to provide you with some of their background information. And, follow up on it. (That includes me!)

What does the source have to gain or lose?

This is especially important when you are on a website that sells a product. If you are taking your information from The Magic Pill Corporation's website and it reports that 99 per cent of patients saw improvement in every aspect of their lives or that some financial website claims that they can increase your profits by 3000 per cent, you have to wonder where they are getting that information. And, you have to wonder what they have to gain by making that claim.

Obviously, The Magic Pill Corporation wants you to buy the magic pill. The investment company wants you to buy their investment products. Why would they report anything other than stellar numbers? It's called: vested interest. So, seek out information that comes from an independent source that has nothing to gain or lose from their report. This doesn't guarantee that bias won't creep in, but it's a better start.

Do other sources agree or disagree?

Once you find information, can you find information that supports it? Can you find information that refutes it? You probably can, and you definitely should. Make it a point to know the various sides to a story and determine which one seems more logically developed.

This will serve two purposes. First, it will give you a lot more knowledge about the topic. This will improve the quality of your presentations. Second, it will allow you to consider tough questions posed by members of the audience, particularly opposing members. Knowing more than what you report is always a good idea. If nothing else, you'll sweat a lot less!

Skepticism — The Key to Finding Good Information

The truth is out there. You just have to look for it. Most of what you find will be worthless and possibly harmful. It is necessary to have a healthy dose of skepticism when reviewing information. Much of what is out there posing as fact are really opinions, and sometimes outright lies.

Finding the truth is a process. It takes time; it takes effort. It's not always fun, but it is always worth it. Ask the tough questions to find the real answers.

Here are a few constructive ways to harness that skepticism, whether you are preparing a speech or just listening to one:

Check for a Source

There is a source for every fact or figure provided. When the speaker does not mention a source, the default source, then, is the speaker. When that occurs, ask yourself, *"How does the speaker know this is true?"* Yes, if you are the speaker, ask yourself how you know this is true. Red flags for undocumented sources include phrases like "statistics show" or "it's a known fact that...."

There had better be a source that follows.

Check the Source Given

So, it's not enough to have a source; you need a *good* source. That is, *you need a source that can be trusted for providing valid and unbiased information.* So, if you are trying to convince us to buy widgets, you don't want to say that "Widgets.com reports that widgets perform 35% better than other leading brands!" Not that *Widgets.com* doesn't have integrity, but they certainly are biased.

By the way, buy my book. According to Mark Woods, it's the best book ever written!

See?

Seek an Alternative

When a speaker discusses a solution to a problem, he will often try to make it sound like that solution is the only viable one. As a critical thinker, *actively seek an alternative solution.* If there's more than one answer, your job is to find it. Why? Because, it will help to expose any weaknesses in the speaker's argument. Note: if you're that speaker, it will give you a chance to address any counter-arguments coming from other critical thinkers in the audience.

Question the Logic

Speakers will develop arguments to persuade audiences to change (e.g. buy a product, adopt a new behavior). They will use any trick in the book to make it seem like a good idea. For example, they will tell you that some authority figure endorses the change, like "Read it; Oprah did!"

But, ultimately, you must ask yourself, *"Will changing benefit the audience or the speaker?"* If it is more of a benefit to the speaker, then it is not a good argument.

Skeptical, But Not Jaded

Question everything, but be sure to do so in the spirit of seeking the truth. Too often the skeptic raises doubt as a means of destroying new ideas rather than refining them. It's too easy to become jaded and bitter toward the world; experience can be a cruel friend. But, take the doubts and seek the truth. Take what's given and make it better.

That will make you a better speaker, a better speechwriter, certainly a better thinker.

RESEARCH SHOWS...

"Research shows that..." or "Statistics show...."

It sure sounds good. Seems like a ton of research went into making those statements, but that's fairly deceptive. As you can see, there's an implication that you looked at dozens of published research studies and synthesized them into some general conclusion. For most speeches, this is probably not the case.

More than likely, you probably found an article that said, "research shows..." and you've decided to make it your own. Let's never mind the potential for plagiarism in this case—unless you are willing to say "According to J. Doe's 2008 article titled 'Blah,' research shows...". Let's instead ask the obvious question: Did the writer look at dozens of published research studies and synthesize them into some general conclusion?

If so, then you should be able to see a reference page about a mile long (or at least with a dozen or so scholarly journal articles). If not, then we have to wonder how the writer can make such a sweeping generalization based on research or statistics.

Some effort to find information was probably done (but I want that reference page or a set of footnotes), but how much? Is the "research" based on one study? Two studies? A dozen studies? A comprehensive look at the literature? One research study or statistic is not proof of anything. But, as more evidence is found, the more support you have to believe in the findings. To say "statistics show" based off one chart is at best irresponsible. To say "statistics show" based off someone else saying "statistics show" is akin to spreading rumors.

Make sure you can back up your "research" with... well, the actual research.

EXPERT OPINIONS ARE STILL JUST OPINIONS

As I listened to a persuasive speech recently, I remember writing my critique. It's a common refrain: where's the evidence? Of course, just as I wrote that, the speaker mentioned some expert's opinion on the matter. I was a bit baffled as it dawned on me that this so-called expert had an opinion without any evidence to back up his assertion.

Are Numbers Any Better?

I'll be the first to say that statistics can be easily manipulated. Any time you see a number reported, you ought to wonder about that number. You also need to wonder about the numbers that are not reported.

But, with numbers, we can (potentially) find the source of information, find the missing numbers, or perhaps find more data that supports or refutes the numbers provided. If there are any perceived flaws with the method of data collection, you could always try to either replicate the study or redesign it so that it is objective and more precise.

The Value and Use of Opinions

But, with an opinion, what can you do? When an expert says, "Chocolate ice cream is the best," about the only three things you can do are:

- agree
- disagree
- ask, "Really?"

Everyone has an opinion. Just because someone has an advanced degree or spent twenty years in the field does not necessarily qualify his or her opinion any more than anyone else, unless research in that field is involved. If you give us a qualified opinion based on research, we can then ask for that research to see if it leads us to the same conclusion. Otherwise, the opinion is no more valid than any other opinion.

Experts in Their Field

My doctor can give me medical advice because she has studied medicine for years and her opinion on certain medical topics is based on research. However, when she tells me that home schooling is not a valid form of education or that students need to wear uniforms because she feels it would help students focus on education instead of fashion… well, she's certainly allowed to think and feel as she pleases, but she's not as studied in the fields of education or sociology.

Quoting her seems like a good idea; that doctor title makes her sound smart and therefore qualified to give her opinion. And, she is smart, but her opinion on non-medical or non-researched topics is just that: an opinion.

How to Handle Expert Opinions

Expert opinions cannot be the stopping point of your research. If the expert says "Studies show...," then find out what studies are doing all this showing. When an expert says, "I think," or "I feel," find out where that thought or feeling originates.

If it's based in research, then find those sources. Then, search for other sources. Do the sources agree or disagree? Is there new information the expert hasn't considered?

If the opinion is based in experience, then realize that this is a limited source; we can't replicate someone's experience nor can we determine how that experience impacted that individual. Someone who witnesses the misuse of charity donations could form a very negative opinion of all charity organizations based on this one unfortunate incident. This experience will have more impact than all the studies that show the positive effects of charity funds correctly used.

Formulate Your Own

Ultimately, the role of the expert is to be the person who has done the research for us and provides us with a way to see that research. They are not there to tell us how to feel. They are there to give us information that will help us to determine what to think or how to feel. To that end, make sure you seek several experts, but more importantly, find the sources from which their opinions come. Then, and only then, formulate your own opinion. You might be surprised to find that by the time you do, you'll be an expert, too.

HOW TO CITE SOURCES IN A SPEECH

Citing a source in a paper is easy. I come from an APA (American Psychological Association) background, so all I have to do is quote some journal article or book and write: "(Woods, 2009)." But, saying that in a speech wouldn't exactly flow: "Open parenthesis Woods two thousand nine page seven closed parenthesis" just sounds weird and takes too long to say.

There must be a way. So, what can you do?

A Sore Cite

First, let's discuss some solutions that just don't work.

Leaving citations out- The classic move of ignoring the problem only magnifies the problem. At best, people will wonder where all your information is coming from. At worst, you may be accused of plagiarism as the audience will think you are trying to claim the language or ideas as your own.

Citing sources at the end- A simple solution to the problem above: put the sources at the end! Unfortunately, the conclusion sounds like this: "And, in conclusion, I got my sources from..." followed by a list of vague sources. Why is this bad? Well, the conclusion is supposed to summarize the relevant information and assess the purpose of the speech, perhaps even urge us to action or provide the next steps. This one sounds like a reference page. That just doesn't work. In addition, we have no idea which facts, figures, and quotes go to which sources. And if you only have one source, you better do some more research!

That leaves us where we started: what can you do?

A Cite for Sore Eyes or Ears

Believe it or not, you can cite a source without disrupting the flow. Page numbers and the year of publication are not necessary, but you can add the name and the title of the work very easily. Observe:

> "Mark Woods, author of 'How to Prepare a Pretty Good Speech,' states that...."

If you quote this author again, simply say:

> "According to Woods...."

Of course, the audience may wonder where in the book you got that quote. It's beyond the speech to provide that, but a reference sheet can be handed out after the speech, or the complete citation can be placed on an overhead slide, perhaps with the quote included.

Is There Such Thing as Too Much Information?

Magazine articles or web pages become a bit more difficult, but again, making mention of the author and the source can still be done:

> "*Literary critic Joan Smith, in a 2008 Writers on Written Stuff magazine article titled 'What's up with Citations?' states....*"

(And, there's no such author, magazine, or article. This was just purely an exercise.)

Yes, it's a lot of information, but it helps to give the audience some background and context. From that point on, you can simply refer to "Smith" and not the article title or the magazine, unless you are quoting her from a different source.

The Effects of Added Effort

Ultimately, it's important to weave in the sources as you speak. It lends a certain credibility to what you are saying through the accuracy (of your work) and by proxy (i.e. the credibility of the sources themselves). Taking the extra time to add the sources may feel like more work, but it's the necessary effort needed to develop a better speech.

Long after the words and the sources are forgotten, it's the impression you make that will be remembered. Be remembered as someone who develops a well-cited, well-developed speech. It's amazing how little things like that can make a big difference over time.

WHY CITE SOURCES IN A SPEECH?

I can think of two simple reasons for citing sources in a speech: credit and credibility. Let's look at them more closely.

Where Credit is Due

Other people work hard to produce a body of work (and by "work," I'm talking about anything that person has produced and had copyrighted). They deserve the recognition.

Whenever you present someone else's work without acknowledging the source, you are essentially claiming that you are the creator of that work. This is known as plagiarism and is illegal (and uncool).

When to Give Credit

When do we cite a source? It's really simple: Cite the source for every fact, idea, or figure (number).

If you hear about something happening in the news, cite the source: "According to the Associated Press...."

Paraphrasing some long passage? That's still someone else's idea (your words, their work). Cite the source.

If you have some number, like a year or quantity, cite the source. "The Weather Channel reports that...."

Some exceptions, of course, include things that are common knowledge. But, determining what that is (like, Columbus sailing for the New World in 1492) is sometimes more difficult than simply finding a source to back up what you vaguely remember from grade school social studies class.

When in doubt, cite a source.

Credibility—Looking Smarter or More Important by Proxy

The other good reason to cite a source is for credibility. We live in a world of experts (so-called). Adding the results of their work will give your presentation a measure of legitimacy. As noted above, omitting the source will not only land you in trouble for plagiarism, it will also call into question the legitimacy of your claims. If you tell us that the H1N1 virus (i.e. the "swine flu") is dangerous, we are not inclined to believe you. However, if you are a medical researcher working for the Center for Disease Control, we are more likely to believe you.

In addition, simply providing your opinions just won't cut it. We want to know what the experts say on the matter. Adding their opinions (for whatever it's truly worth) will add a degree of credibility to your speech or presentation. So, your opinion on a book is no less valid than Oprah Winfrey's opinion, but millions of fans trust her to choose great books to read. Whether or not she is truly an authority on books can be debated, but her influence on others cannot. So, if she says a book is terrific, and you agree, then use her as a source within your speech. Seems silly, but it works.

Add sources to your speeches and presentations and notice the impact it has on others. You put yourself on the right side of the law and you impress others. That's win-win baby!

CHAPTER 6

DELIVERING THE SPEECH

DELIVER MORE IMPACT

Even if you follow the advice given on how to quickly improve as a speaker, your speech can still fall flat. Something is lost in the translation, and you sense it, even if you can't completely identify it. The topic is relevant. The research is comprehensive. The format is fluid. What's the problem?

The words are important, and that's why it is so crucial for you to get to the point and say only what needs to be said. The ideas are important in terms of choosing the right topic for the right audience and making sure you know both inside and out.

But what about how you say what needs to be said?

Where's the Feeling? Where's the Love?

Part of the problem is that you aren't considering how your delivery impacts the audience. Think about some of your favorite songs. The singer pours out emotion in each note and in every word. She makes you feel what she is feeling through her performance.

Now consider when you sing "Happy Birthday" to your co-workers: mumbling the words, hoping not to be heard, and wishing the cake would get cut and passed around without having to sing that song. Imagine if your favorite singer sang your favorite song the way you just sang to your co-worker. You probably wouldn't consider either your favorite for very long, would you?

No one is asking you to put on some kind of concert performance (though, if you really want to have an impact... I'm just saying...), but there are a few things you can do to make your words have an impact on the audience. It starts with wanting to have an impact. The rest of it consists of a few items for your consideration:

Believe in what you say To get some feeling into your speech, it helps to actually care about what you have to say. If you want to have an impact on others, caring about them enough to believe in the message is a good way to start.

Speak, don't read For whatever reason, we have a reading voice that sounds like we're trying to make sure no actual emotion sneaks out. Why is that? I'm not entirely sure, but the reasons aren't important. What you need to realize is that if you read your speech (and many speakers do), you can't *sound* like you're reading. Audiences know the difference between someone who is speaking to them and someone who is reading in front of them. You'll always have more of an impact on someone who feels like you are talking to them.

Stress important words Notice above how the word *sound* is in italics. You can't actually hear me speaking to you since this is written, but the italics imply that the word is somehow stressed for effect. I wanted you to know that the word was of particular importance. The italics served as a visual cue. You can do that with your voice, whether it's changing the pitch, drawing the word out a little longer, pausing just before you say the stressed word, or anything that puts extra attention to the word you stressed. Such vocal variety will provide richness to what you are saying.

Measure your words I watched a performer recently say to the judges, "Thank you so much. I love you so much. I'm so excited to be here; I want this so much." I'm not asking you to define how much "so much" is, but I do caution you to think about making such vague or empty statements. And, beware of making such comments over and over again. Saying "you know what I'm saying?" at the end of each sentence gets quickly annoying, and the audience will begin to tune out.

Choose better words Some words have more meaning than others. Some words are more colorful. Use these words to create images that are clearly imagined by your audience. Notice that distinction; don't use a thesaurus to find different words for the sake of being different or to try and sound smarter. Use words that will have an impact on the audience. Notice terms like "corporate restructuring" were developed to soften the blow of people losing jobs, or shareholders losing money. Saying something is "unwise" or "plain stupid" can mean the same thing, but it certainly will call up different emotions.

Lively face, lively voice It's really strange, but try putting on a big smile on your face and then try to sound sad or angry or anything other than happy or peppy. Granted, the peppiness may seem sarcastic, but it is extremely difficult to make sounds that are inconsistent with your facial expression. So, it stands to reason that if we keep a blank expression on our faces while speaking, we'll probably have a fairly blank tone in our voices. Add emotion by simply smiling or frowning. Your facial expressions can reveal what you feel inside, and it gets translated in how you say what you say.

You Already Do It, So Do It Already

The funny thing about all of this is that you already do all of this without really thinking about it. You are expert speakers when you talk to your friends or colleagues. You understand and employ all of these tactics for the purpose of having a greater or lesser impact. But, for whatever reason, you decide to throw out these skills when you give a speech or presentation—just when you need it the most!

This isn't a lesson so much as it is a reminder to use what you already have to deliver more of an impact on your audience. The results will amaze you… and the audience as well.

THE SOLUTION FOR EYE CONTACT

How important is eye contact? I know a lot of speakers wish eye contact wasn't important. But, if you think about having a casual conversation with anyone, you have an expectation that the person will look at you. What happens when she doesn't?

You start to think odd thoughts. You wonder if that person is hiding something. You wonder if they are outright lying to you. You wonder if they are bored with you or if they have some sort of social issue. Something must be wrong.

You'll notice that whatever you are wondering becomes far more important than anything being said. You probably didn't even hear what was said because you were lost in thought.

Well, this happens to audiences as well. On some level, they will wonder why you aren't looking up at them, missing that crucial connection with the audience. They will continue to dwell on this issue or else they will simply shrug and pay attention to something else or someone else. At this point, your message, however important, is lost.

Poor Excuses for Eye Contact

You understand that eye contact is important, but you do these weird things that stand in for eye contact without actually being eye contact. Let me see if I can list them:

- looking at the wall behind the audience
- looking up once or twice the entire speech
- looking up every two seconds at no one in particular
- looking at only one person the entire speech (creepy!)
- looking up while keeping your eyes on the paper

I'm sure there are other little tricks, but these are the most obvious. It looks like you are making an attempt at eye contact without having to make eye contact. It's almost like you are saying to the audience, "I hope you appreciate effort instead of eye contact. It's the best I can do."

Sorry, but pseudo-eye contact is just not the same as real eye contact.

How to Look at the Audience

Looking at the audience is an art unto itself. It helps to look at them from the perspective of someone who is trying to help a friend in need. That will help when it comes time to face them. But, that's not really the same as connecting your gaze with theirs. How do you do that?

Sweep across the room connecting with individuals. Don't go row by row, person by person, making eye contact. Mix it up. Look at someone to the left, then move across and someone to the right, then someone in the back. Give everyone a random opportunity to meet your gaze. Individuals who are singled out will become uncomfortable if you keep looking only at them or more than anyone else. Others will also begin to feel as if you aren't addressing them if you don't provide eye contact.

Inevitably, you will probably move toward the friendlier faces, and when you move back and forth across the audience, you might find yourself drawn to their face. This is acceptable; just try to remember that everyone deserves a chance to make that connection with you. Not everyone will want it, but everyone needs that opportunity.

Of course, you will look away, either at your notes or somewhere beyond the audience. Again, this is natural. There's no need to lock your gaze upon the audience unceasingly.

It's Just a Conversation... With Lots More People

Ultimately, keep in mind that you are talking to someone, or rather a group of some ones, all of whom have expectations similar to a personal one-on-one conversation. The standard rules apply: look at them, but not too long. Look around a bit, but always come back to them.

Smile a little. Care about them. Give them your best.

Okay, maybe that's not eye contact, but it's still contact, and without it, eye contact becomes a bit cold. Be sure to be warm.

METHODS OF DELIVERY—THE MANUSCRIPT

There are basically four ways to deliver a speech:

- manuscript—write it out entirely
- memorize it
- wing it (i.e. impromptu)
- use notes or brief outline

Each of these methods of delivery has its advantages and disadvantages. Be sure to note your strengths and weaknesses when determining a method of delivery.

Using the Manuscript—Advantages

Writing out a speech in its entirety is fairly common in my experience. On the surface, it seems to be the best method:

- you know exactly what you want to say
- you can really develop the format
- you can choose your words more carefully

A lot of my students have a tremendous amount of anxiety stemming from a fear of the unknown. Maybe we all suffer from this to some extent. It's bad enough that you have to look at all those people looking back at you. No sense in compounding the problem by not knowing what to say. That makes sense. Write out the speech, and you automatically make this a less daunting task.

When you write out the speech, you can really focus on the format. It's nice to write down "introduction," "body," and "conclusion" and begin the process of filling in the blank spaces. It's nice to go back and see what's working and what's not working. It's nice to be able to add in quotes or numbers or testimony and the sources in a manner that flows from one thought to the next.

It's also nice to go back and edit what has been written, choosing better words or phrases, checking each sentence for clarity, cutting out unnecessary words or statements. Each word can be carefully chosen to provide a bigger impact. The quality of the speech increases with each revision.

In sum, the speech looks and feels more prepared, and probably because it is more prepared (than say, winging it). So, write it out, get up there, and just read it.

But, therein lies some problems.

Are You Speaking Through a Synthesizer?

When you read, you sound like you're reading. I'm not sure what that is, but it has a very washed out, emotionless, monotone quality to it. You don't have to sound that way, but you do. Most of us do. It's like somewhere in sixth or seventh grade we realized that people were judging us for having fun in school, so we quickly acted like we didn't care about doing a better job than others. So, we took all emotion out of our speech, and we muttered and mumbled our way through speeches and acted like we couldn't care less. Everyone else did it, so it must be the right thing to do, right? Not so much.

Why Won't You Look at Me?

Not only do we sound like we're reading when we read, but we are actually reading, or rather we are not engaging the audience. Eye contact suffers tremendously. It's terribly difficult to read something and look at something else (or someone else). If you actually do look up, you run the risk of losing your place and your rhythm.

What Did I Write?

One problem with reading a speech aloud is that it requires a certain degree of expectation. You almost need to know what you are going to say before you say it. I realize that you think that writing it is enough to jog your memory when it comes to reading the speech to an audience. But, how many times have you read something aloud only to get confused by the wording? For whatever reason, the word order just doesn't make sense to you, and you end up staring at the page trying to figure out what the heck you wrote the other day.

Word Processors?

Another problem with reading a speech is that it requires you to write it out. That's time-consuming. This isn't so much a problem by itself, except that a lot of people (at least a lot of my students) seem to handwrite the speeches. This wouldn't be an issue if everyone printed in nice big letters and in a clear, consistent font. But, this isn't the case.

No, instead, I have seen speeches written on the back of old tests, notebook paper, and even on a napkin. Ever the thrifty ones, the words are scratched onto the paper in a 5-pt. font that can only be described as "chicken-scratch-vitica." I rather enjoy watching them squint at their own writing and wonder what it means.

It means type it out with a word processor. It means make it a nice large (i.e. readable) font.

The Solution?

All these problems suggest that maybe you ought to choose a different method of delivery. That might work, but let's not be too hasty. You can work from a manuscript (or any method). The key is to recognize the problems associated with the manuscript, and work harder to overcome them.

That means you will have to spend more time working on the delivery of the speech, particularly on the sound of your voice and the eye contact with the audience. For your voice, you'll have to bring back some feeling in what you say. It helps to know what you are saying, and actually feel tied to what you are saying. In other words, you'll have to read the speech aloud several times, practicing how you say the words. As for eye contact, you have to find ways to really look at your audience. We'll look at that more in-depth later, but for now, understand the need to make that connection with other people with their eyes (and yours).

So, by simply taking the time to practice your well-written speech, you'll understand it enough to deliver it with more impact. By taking the time to write it out clearly (whether on index cards or with a word processor), you stand a better chance of not getting confused by what you read.

METHODS OF DELIVERY—SPEAKING FROM MEMORY

You might be thinking that the manuscript method is just too difficult to pull off because of the lack of eye contact. I don't blame you. It's really difficult to read and look at other people at the same time. In fact, that's just about impossible. Instead, you look up just enough to make sure you lose your place reading every time. The fun never starts.

Read It from Your Mind

So, the obvious solution is to write it out, memorize it, and then recite it from memory. This has two distinct advantages:

Improved eye contact   You can actually look at people as if you were talking to them.

No reading voice   Much like an actor, you can now perform the speech rather than simply read it to the audience. You'll sound far more dynamic (if you want to).

Start the Song on the Second Line of the Second Verse

Of course, there are drawbacks to this method. They revolve around the fact that our ability to recall has diminished over time as individuals and as a society. We just aren't required to jam a lot of information into our heads for extended periods of time. But, this leads to problems if you choose to memorize a speech.

The lack of persistence of memory   It's hard to remember a list of three or four grocery items. If I don't write it down, I'll inevitably forget one of those items. Imagine that happening to you in the middle of a speech; you simply blank on a word or a portion of the speech. Well, it could happen, and that's just added stress you simply don't need.

Getting knocked off rhythm Sometimes we simply forget what's next because we get out of rhythm. Someone raises her hand to ask a question or simply blurts something out and you get stopped from delivering your speech. And for some reason, you can't remember what the next thing to say is; you lost the rhythm. It's like having someone ask you to sing a song starting from somewhere other than the beginning. You almost have to sing it in your mind before you can get to the line you want to start. Many a good speech can get derailed this way.

Extra work Let's be honest; you wrote out the speech, so you have a manuscript. That's a lot of work. Now, you add the extra step of committing it to memory. You've essentially doubled your workload. How many times will you be giving this speech? If it is only once, is it really worth the bother of memorizing?

Is It Worth It?

So, maybe the memorization of speeches just isn't the best method. It's hard to do; it requires a lot of work for a little gratification.

Of course, if you plan to give the same speech over and over (such as a sales pitch or as part of a speaking series), this might be worth the investment. It's more than likely that as you give this speech repeatedly, you'll begin to remember more and more of it.

METHODS OF DELIVERY—WINGING IT (IMPROMPTU STYLE)

So, we've established that memorizing speeches is not fun. Too much work, too little gain. Also, there's just too much room for error. And, that "work" thing just doesn't sound like fun.

Maybe you can just wing it.

Impromptu Doesn't Really Mean "Winging It"

I've been a bit cavalier about the impromptu method of speaking. I've referred to it as "winging it," but that's a bit of an overstatement. Impromptu speeches require as much rigorous research and development as any other method of delivery. It might even require more because of the uncertainty of the time and place and even the subject of the speech. You have to be ready to speak at all times. That means you have to plan for the unexpected.

Expert Status Required

In order to be really good at this method of delivery, you need to do a lot of research in a particular field. It stands to reason that you ought to be an expert in your field of choice (such as your career or industry or product). You need to know it inside and out. You need to spend time reading up on the latest information (new techniques, new insights). Find out what others are doing or thinking. Be able to quote them. Understand any controversies or debates in your field.

Then, and only then, you will have enough information stored away to attempt an impromptu speech.

Making a Real Connection

Of course, since you are so well-versed in our method of developing a speech, this method of delivery will be second-nature. There are advantages to speaking in this manner:

> *Truly engaged with the audience* Unlike the manuscript or reciting from memory, you are truly talking to the audience. They will, as a result, feel far more a part of the event than an audience listening to someone reading at them. They will be more inclined to ask questions and be involved in the discussion.
>
> *Far livelier delivery* Again, there's nothing more engaging to an audience than someone who is talking to them and not reading at them. Your facial expressions will be far more genuine. That quality will find its way into your voice as well.

Increased credibility This comes from being an expert and being able to display that expertise. When you know your subject matter well enough that you don't need to write it out, yet you can still deliver it in a clear format, you will be far more impressive to the audience.

All that Flapping Will Make You Sweat

Some speakers think that it's much easier just to get up there and see what happens. This is not truly an impromptu speech; it really is just winging it on a hope and a prayer. Unfortunately, the results are usually disastrous. The word "um" becomes just a tad overused (if a million times equals a "tad"). Formatting is not the hallmark of this ill prepared speech. In fact, the words "random" or "ramble" come to mind.

If you enjoy a good, cold sweat from knowing that everything you are saying is confusing, useless, and possibly annoying, then by all means, wing that speech. Or, if you are someone who is oblivious to how an audience feels about your fourteen minute diatribe on how your cousin owes you fifteen bucks and you love singing karaoke music, enjoy yourself. Don't be surprised, though, if you don't get that sale or promotion—or a decent grade in class.

METHODS OF DELIVERY—USING BRIEF NOTES

What if there was a way you could incorporate the best of the other methods of delivery while minimizing the worst of the other methods? Yes, it's called the *extemporaneous method* of delivery, which is a fancy way of saying that you use brief notes or an outline.

How It's Done

There is no real wrong way to do this. Simply write out the parts that you feel need careful wording and place words or phrases where you need a reminder but otherwise know the material really well.

For example, you might decide that an introduction needs a certain degree of formality and precision, so you would write out everything from the attention-getter to the preview of main points. However, for the body, you know the main points fairly well, so instead of writing it out, you simply list the three main points, maybe writing out the example you want to use or the source and quote you want to add to a particular main point.

A Simple Example

Let's say you are introducing an old friend to a group or club you belong to. You've been asked to give a formal introduction of your friend. Well, you know this guy really well, so you don't need much, but you do want to have some of the basics down for your speech. No problem:

> *Attention-getter*   Once or twice in life, you get the opportunity to meet someone truly special and form a bond that cannot be severed.
>
> *Introduce topic*   For me—for all of us—that would be my friend, Bob (or Jane).
>
> *Preview of main points*   Background, hobbies, goals
>
> *Purpose*   Welcome to the club
>
> *Body*
>
> *Background*   how we met, college, occupation, career highlights
>
> *Hobbies*   Basketball, swimming, camping (tell camping story)
>
> *Goal*   Make contribution to this club

You don't have to write anything out entirely; just use these notes to give you the basic format of the speech and a few reminders of what you want to discuss, and you have a pretty good speech outlined to give.

Organic... (Somewhat) but Planned... (Somewhat)

Speaking extemporaneously allows you quite a bit of freedom while giving you definite direction. Following are the basic advantages to using this method of delivery.

Engagement Using these brief notes will allow you all the liveliness of the impromptu method without sacrificing the rigorous formatting of the manuscript. Eye contact is also improved, naturally.

Recall You won't have to worry about losing your place while reading because there are only brief notes for you to use to jog your memory. Notice how much our memory improves when we have a few clues to help us!

Structure This style will sound more like you are talking to the audience, but with more opportunity to structure the speech. You can plan better where you want the speech to go while still accounting for inevitable bumps in the road.

Accuracy By writing out more difficult parts (such as quotes or numbers and their sources), you won't have to be quite the expert that the impromptu speaker does, but you'll sound like one.

Only One Drawback?

Of course, if there was any disadvantage to this method, it comes from repeated engagements. Because you are using words that come top of mind, you might not always word things correctly. There will still be times where the dreaded "ums" will appear, usually where you have only one or two words to jog your memory.

This method, however, is still the best way to deliver a speech (yes, I'm biased on this one). It gives you every opportunity to really talk to the audience while giving you a definitive road map to lead them. Over time, you'll find that you will be able to connect with the audience more intimately without having the anxiety attacks of not knowing what to say.

Besides, why be afraid? It's only a speech, right?

OVERCOMING YOUR FEAR

What are we afraid of? Why do we tighten up at the thought of getting in front of people and speaking? I had someone tell me once that it was because of "all of those eyeballs" just staring at you. That is kind of weird when you really think about it, but it goes deeper than that.

Maybe it's a fear of failure. That seems to make sense. Our society praises the winners and forgets the also-rans. John McCain and the Cardinals share more than the home state of Arizona; they will share the special distinction of being forgotten for almost making it to the top. And, maybe that's a blessing.

The Root of Fear

While failure certainly hurts, I don't know that it is the driving force of our fear. How often have we quietly failed as we learn new skills? Ever notice how a toddler learning to stand and walk will fall repeatedly without incident? It's only when the child notices you watching that tears and screams of pain result. How could a dozen spills without tears suddenly change when someone notices? I doubt the fall hurt any worse than the others. Something else is at play- the perceived judgment coming from others.

Failure, then, is not something we fear; it's failing in front of others that makes us quake. No one wants to look or feel stupid.

Judge Not (Yourself or Others)

Here's the part that really stings: it's not coming from others, it's coming from you. As mentioned earlier, you can never really know what others truly think or feel. However, you can know how *you* feel.

And how *do* you feel?

If I had to guess, I'd say you feel that being successful is very important. Looking stupid (i.e. failing in front of others) is intolerable. And, if you think this way, others must surely think this way, too.

In effect, you are now faced with an impossible situation. Which is more important: succeeding or not failing? Is it worth the risk of looking like an idiot for the possibility of looking good? Most people think not.

But, it comes down to the idea that you created this situation. People are just sitting there looking at you. Some of them are hoping for an entertaining or useful presentation. Others are wondering what they are going to eat for dinner tonight or text messaging their friends about the weekend. However, you assume they are sitting there judging you. Why?

I think it comes back to the idea of not judging others ("judge not, lest you be judged"). This is a powerful statement. It means that judging others leads to reactive judgment from others. Call me stupid? You're stupid! But, less understood is the idea that if you make a judgment, it will actually limit your potential. Let's say, for example that you say that people from the 1970s wearing bell-bottom jeans looked foolish. Your judgment now makes it impossible for you to wear bell-bottoms (and they seem to make comebacks every 10 years or so) without others saying, "Hey! I thought you said it was foolish-looking? Why are you wearing them?"

Now you have to eat your words.

Now, take that into the world of public speaking. Someone gets up and speaks and is red-faced and stuttering and you laugh a little and think, "What a fool! Glad I'm not him!" But, then it's your turn, and suddenly, you've made it unacceptable to feel flushed and to stutter.

It's a World You Create

If you think the world sits in judgment of others, it's probably because you do it. So, if you stop thinking harshly about other people's mistakes, yours become a little easier to forgive. You don't have to worry about what others think, and you don't have to worry about what you think. You don't have to hold yourself up to standards that are impossible to achieve. Believe me; you aren't perfect. I'll save you the trouble of trying to figure that out. You will make mistakes. So will everyone else.

Realizing that we aren't perfect, maybe we can focus on the important things instead of all the little mistakes we made, make, or will make. Maybe if you choose to believe that it's okay, you can get to the business of succeeding instead of not failing. When you measure success in the positive impact your message has on others and not on your ability to minimize your apparent foolishness, then you will begin the process of overcoming your fear of public speaking.

DON'T HIDE BEHIND VISUAL AIDS

Visual aid (typically multi-media overhead projection, aka PowerPoint presentations) can enhance a speech, but more often than not, it is generally used as either a crutch for the speaker or else a way to hide from the audience. Neither is particularly effective. Remember, the message is the most important aspect of the speech, and the impact on the audience from that message is the ultimate goal. If your visual aid isn't helping to enhance the message, then it is working against your purpose.

So, if you must use visual aid, here are some simple rules to keep in mind. They will help you to develop more effective presentations.

Talk to the audience, not to the screen

A visual presentation is meant to enhance the speech, not to be the speech. Do not write out your entire speech onto a series of slides and then proceed to read from the screen. That's not visual aid, at least not for the audience. Again, this seems like a clever way to keep from looking at the audience and for the audience to keep from looking at you, but this is not a win-win situation. No one will be impressed with the visuals, and certainly no one will be excited by the prospect of looking at the back of your head for the entire presentation.

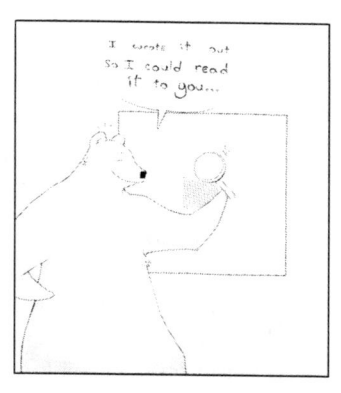

Keep it simple and easy to read

Since we've already established that you can't write out your entire speech, you need to keep it simple:

- bullet points—key words
- 3-4 bullets per screen
- dark background, bright font
- sans serif font, 18pt or higher

Simple pictures and graphs are okay—no gimmicks

I know there's this urge to jazz up the presentation. This usually comes in several annoying forms—moving words, sound effects, and moving pictures.

Moving words At first blush, it seems so cool. Words are flying all over the place or spinning into view or being sprayed onto the screen like bullets. But, you'll soon realize that, while the effect seems cool, it's all very time-consuming and distracting. The speaker usually has to stop and wait for the words to finish gyrating as the audience focuses on the motion and not on the speaker's voice.

Sound effects Usually tied to the moving words, we get to hear them swishing or swooshing or shooting in. Again, it doesn't take much to distract an audience. The weird sounds will do just that. They also distract the speaker. Any sound not coming from the speaker is competition to the speaker. And, believe me; the effects get old after the first two or three.

Moving pictures This is less time-consuming, but just as distracting. It seems like a great idea to have a blinking question mark or a cartoon truck driving down a road, but this is really the equivalent to a blinking neon sign. It attracts attention, and usually the wrong kind.

Honestly, any of these effects conveys the wrong message. It says that your presentation is too weak to stand on its own, that you need these tricks to keep the audience paying attention. In the end, however, they are really just paying attention to the movement or sound and not to you.

Leave it up long enough to understand

Since you are using bullet points and key words, you don't need to keep it up for an especially long time, but at least long enough to comprehend. This is especially true if you are presenting charts or diagrams. Typically, your speech should cover what is being seen, so allow the audience a moment to tie together what you are saying to what they are seeing.

Make sure the technology works

How many times have you gotten to a site to present your work only to find that the projector is out or the computer won't read your flash drive? If you know you are going to speak, make sure you have several access channels to your presentation (put it on a flash drive, email it to yourself, have printed versions of the slides) and test everything before your presentation.

Keep going if something goes wrong

Visual aid is there to enhance the presentation. You should still be able to do an effective job without it. So, if the equipment breaks down (overhead bulbs burn out, computers go down), be ready to keep going. Standing there confused and silent will do nothing to enhance your speech. Laugh it off, make a comment about it, and just keep going.

Use as few visual aids as possible

I know it can be tempting to add fifty charts or pictures. Sometimes you want to do it because you hope to keep the audience occupied, which we've already discussed is a bad idea. However, there are times where you feel the audience needs every piece of information possible. Quite noble, but this will certainly lead to an information overload. Since the audience needs time and explanation to understand the visual aids, fewer is generally better. One or two key charts will do more to have an impact on an audience than thirty or forty charts that will inevitably blur together.

All these rules are calling basically for the same thing: a clear, simple, and effective presentation. Make it easy for them to understand and they will be far more engaged and receptive to your message.

HANDLE THE HANDOUTS

Handouts of the slides, a packet of information, or a set of pictures for the group to look at all seem like such good ideas. You have people looking at something else instead of you. That takes the pressure off. From the perspective of a speaker who would rather not be speaking, this makes sense. But from the perspective of a speaker who is trying to have an impact on the audience, this is a poor strategy.

Shuffle and Bustle of Handouts

Have you ever received handouts during a presentation or a lecture? Did you put them away and focus only on the speaker? Did you follow along with the speaker carefully, taking notes along the way? Well, maybe you did, but more than likely, you probably received your handout, and then handed the rest to someone else to pass along. Then, you and everyone else proceeded to thumb through it to see what was in it. If it was a packet containing the PowerPoint slides to be shown, you probably looked at the slides to get a sense of how long the presentation was going to last. Or, do I exaggerate?

Let's say you are that rare individual that actually takes the handout and follows the speaker carefully. Your attention is still split between the handout and the speaker. That means the speaker is now competing with her own materials for your attention. Your attention gets further diminished with each page you turn ahead. You are further distracted by others flipping through pages of material.

Paying Attention to Her BFF

It's bad enough that, as a speaker, you have to deal with a host of new distractions for audience members. Text messaging and hand held video games are competition enough. They are small enough not to be a distraction to others, though it's still very obvious when you hear messages buzzing in every twenty seconds and the distinct, rapid clicking of buttons as thumbs fire off text messages almost as quickly as one could talk.

Don't give your audience something else to distract them. I know it seems counter-intuitive to you, but you really do want those eyes focused on you. It's the best way for the audience to receive the message for maximum impact. Handouts would just be one more thing to take away from the message (the message from you, not the text message from their BFF—best friend forever, apparently).

Speak First, Hand Out Later

Hand out material after the presentation. The message you bring is the most important thing and must come from you. Anything else (visual aid or handouts) is supplemental information. Handouts are great, but they are just that: supplemental. The speaker will have the greatest impact on the audience; the handouts just help to remind them later of what was discussed.

CHAPTER 7

PUBLIC SPEAKING AND BEYOND

WANTING AND WORKING TO BE A GREAT SPEAKER

It's a simple formula: want it; work for it. Never give up on either, and you are bound to succeed at just about anything.

A student recently told me that she had no intention of ever being a public speaker much less a good speaker. She told me that she didn't have it in her to get up and speak in front of people, and it really doesn't matter. She also said that there was nothing wrong with that.

I couldn't disagree more.

Your Future Is as You Imagine

We walk around with labels: some given to us, some we've assigned. Some of them are good, some of them not so good.

- "She's the athlete in the family."
- "He's a party animal!"
- "I'm just not good with words."

These labels can often be useful; they help us get a sense of self and a sense of others. But, there are problems. Labels are limiting, self-fulfilling, and hold some assumed stereotypes that often go unspoken but understood. If you are called an athlete your whole life, you will be expected to involve yourself in athletics to the exclusion of other endeavors. You will begin to think of yourself as an athlete and only an athlete, and behave in a manner consistent with athletes.

The label defines your future, and thus places limits on your potential.

What if you want something more or even something else? Athletes can enjoy education just as much as a professor can enjoy athletics. The limits are only in your expectations, based on your belief in labels.

Limited by Your Own Beliefs

This brings us back to public speaking. You've labeled yourself as someone who isn't good at it, so you shy away from it. You get nervous and agitated when forced to speak in front of others. Each time you finish, it reinforces in your mind that public speaking is just not for you.

Maybe someone told you that you didn't do a great job and it discouraged you. You believed them and decided it wasn't your thing. Again, labels are so limiting.

Maybe it was a bad first experience. You tried to get up in front of a group and you fell flat on your face. People laughed and you felt silly and stupid. You hated it so much and vowed never to feel that way again.

No matter how you got here, you are convinced that you are a bad speaker. As a result, you don't want to get involved with public speaking. Rather, you want to avoid public speaking. You then actively involve yourself in staying away from it. Wanting and working: you want to avoid public speaking and you work at it. You probably are very good at avoiding it now.

Do What Successful People Do

But you are now limited by this. Your avoidance has moved you into places that don't require public speaking skills. But worse, it's moved you away from things you might enjoy but require public speaking skills. Professional athletes have to speak in front of cameras on a regular basis. Business executives give presentations to groups, large and small, on a regular basis. Actually, just about every successful person has to use public speaking skills on a regular basis.

One of the reasons you notice these successful people is because they are engaging an audience.

If you want that, too, then you're half way there. Next comes the work.

Want It, Work for It

Public speaking is hard work. It takes time. It takes study. It takes practice. You have to make a lot of mistakes. You will fumble over words. You will say the wrong thing. You will forget what to say. You will look like an idiot. Over and over again this will occur. But, slowly, almost imperceptibly, you will begin to make fewer mistakes. You will begin to feel less mortified by these mistakes. You might even learn to laugh about them. And, pretty soon, you'll start to get noticed for your efforts. Opportunities will soon follow.

It all starts with what you want, and it continues with how much you work. Give it enough time and effort, and before you know it, someone will label you as a natural speaker. "Oh, she's a born public speaker."

Yes, it's a label—a self-fulfilling one at that. But it might just be the one label that speaks to limitless possibilities.

EXPAND BEYOND THE BASICS

Now you've got a good idea on how a speech is developed. You have the basics of the introduction, the body, and the conclusion down. You can whip up a speech in about two minutes without even thinking.

And, that's when the trouble starts.

The problem with the basics is that... well, it's basic. It's a good starting point, but the next step is needed. I've heard too many speeches that sound like they were written during class. It's great that thoughts can be quickly transferred to paper and organized (somewhat) well, but not a lot of thought goes into the speech, and it is fairly evident. Allow me to demonstrate with...

The Bumblebee Speech

I'm not proud of this speech, and if you're impressed by it, then I'm a little concerned. But, this speech illustrates the problems of "whipping up" a speech. Observe:

> "Good afternoon. Did you like bumblebees? Well, I do, and today I'm going to tell you about bumblebees. I'll talk about what colors bumblebees are, the sound a bumblebee makes, and whether or not a bumblebee can fly.
>
> First off, bumblebees are black and yellow.
>
> Second, bumblebees make a buzzing sound.
>
> Now that we've established the sound a bumblebee makes, let's find out if a bumblebee can fly. The answer is: yes! Bumblebees can fly.
>
> So, in conclusion, we've looked at the color of bumblebees, the sound they make, and answered the mystery of whether or not bumblebees can fly. So, the next time you see a bumblebee, you can remember these important facts. Thank you."

Good gravy.

What's So Wrong About It?

Can you see what the problems are in this speech? On a technical level, the speech is acceptable. It has (almost) all the parts: the introduction, body, and conclusion. The introduction has an attention-getter, introduction of the topic, and preview of main points. The body includes the main points and transitions between main points. The conclusion summarizes the main points and even provides a purpose or next step.

Sounds good, right? Well, it's not what's in the speech that's wrong; it's what's missing from the speech.

What's Missing?

It's a simple question, and when you look at the answers, you start to see the problems. We're missing:

Utility Notice at the end of the speech, there's an attempt to provide some purpose for the information, but even still, is there any relevant use for it? Who will say, "I remember a speech about bumblebees that said they were black and yellow. The speaker was so right!"

Necessity Very much tied to the utility, there's no sense that this speech is necessary. This particular speech is easy to notice in terms of its uselessness, but others are a little more difficult. In fact, all speeches start out as useless. The speaker has to bring in the need for this information. Why are we listening to this? The audience wants an answer, and a good one.

Credibility This speech requires absolutely no research beyond going outside in the spring or summer months and looking at a bumblebee. Your audience will only look at you as a resource if you show that you have more knowledge on a topic than they do.

Sources Part of doing your research is putting it on a display. Part of gaining credibility is using trusted sources to back up any claims you make. Simply asserting a bumblebee can fly might be enough for this speech, but that should be a clue that the topic is weak. Any fact, figure, quote, or claim you make has to have a source behind it. I suppose saying, "in my opinion" constitutes a source, but that's where the issue of credibility comes back at you. Look for a source, and then look for a better source.

New information Does anybody not know that bumblebees are black and yellow, make a buzzing sound, and can fly? I suppose it's possible, but I'd really like to meet the person who is blown away by these paradigm-shifting facts about bumblebees.

Effort When someone does the minimum to get by and expects the maximum in return, what do you call that? I don't really know for sure. But, I can say that in public speaking, you get from the audience what you give to the audience. Give them the least, and you get the least in return.

It seems like a lot of work, and it is. Public speaking, like anything else, takes time to develop. It takes work. Can people cut corners and slide by doing very little? Yes, they can, but what does that get you?

Don't Get Good at Being Bad

At first, it seems like it gets you out of a lot of unnecessary work. But, over time, it becomes a skill (and a pretty useless one). You always get really good at the things you do over and over again. If you cut corners and avoid work, you'll get really good at it. The problem is, nobody wants to hire people who are good at avoiding work. That just makes more work for others.

Take the Extra Steps

Take the time to expand beyond the basics of public speaking. Think about your topic and how it impacts the audience. Do your research to make sure you have the best information to give to them. Give them your sources so they can build trust in you. Give them new information so that the experience (i.e. the speech) has value. Put in the effort so that you get more even as you give more.

It really is the formula for success– in public speaking and in any endeavor.

APPLYING SKILLS BEYOND THE OBVIOUS

I went to a poetry reading recently and was thrilled to see a student of mine read one of his poems. Everything was great except that he broke one of my rules of public speaking; he finished with "that's it."

I asked him in shock, "How could you break Rule #2?" He looked at me in mild surprise and laughed.

"I didn't know this was supposed to be like a speech," he said.

That's when I realized that we often fail to apply what we've learned to different situations. Making sure to never say "that's it" at the end of a speech seems to only apply to speeches given in class only. The rules stop at the door.

What does that mean, though? These rules aren't arbitrarily placed. They aren't hoops to jump through for the duration of class to be discarded upon turning in the final exam... are they?

Applications and Priorities

These "rules" and principles of public speaking were developed for you to apply to every situation that can gain you an advantage. Why would you go out of your way to prepare a great persuasive speech for a class, but then fail to prepare for a job interview? The speech might be worth ten per cent of your grade for that class while that interview might be the key to your career aspirations. Why spend a week working on that speech (which you should, don't get me wrong), but then decide to "wing it" for the most important interview of your career?

It doesn't add up.

Measuring Your Education

The true measure of your education will be how well you can apply whatever skills you have learned to new and different situations. Ask yourself how any skill you acquire can be used in different situations to give you an advantage. Being a leader on the football field doesn't have to end after the game is over. Those skills can serve you well in the boardroom or in a group or community project. Likewise, being skilled in persuasive communication doesn't have to be just for a speech class. These same skills can help you interview well for that job you want or to convince potential customers or clients to purchase your product or service.

So, I repeat: the true measure of your education will be how you apply whatever skills you have developed to new and different situations. Figuring out how you can do that *is* your education. The result you get serves as the measure of how well you learned, and is more gratifying than any letter grade given in any classroom.

MAKE IT BETTER

I've tried to take what I've learned since my first book and make it better. I hope that you will be able to do the same. There's so much that goes into being a success, and I've tried to demonstrate to you what role public speaking plays in your success. So far, I've tried to expand beyond simply showing you how to prepare a speech or utilizing the skills to get a job, a promotion, or a better grade. It's so much more than that. It's a way of seeing the world and how you fit within it.

1. It's a world of people with needs.
2. You have a skill set:
   - the ability to gather meaningful information or develop meaningful arguments
   - the ability to synthesize and organize that information or those arguments
   - the ability to provide what is needed to an audience in an effective and elegant manner

Success in whatever you choose comes from recognizing that this world of people with needs will benefit from your set of skills. Provide for them, and you will find what you're looking for, whether it is financial rewards, social accolades, or even spiritual fulfillment. My guess is that you might just find all three.

You have it within you to be great public speakers or to use the skills you've acquired to be great successes. If you apply these skills, you'll get pretty good at them (maybe you already have). But I urge you to take what you have and make it better.

Ask yourselves:

- how can I make it better?
- how can I make this sentence, this point, this introduction, this speech better?
- how can I make other people's lives better?
- how can I make this world better?

You can. You really can.

MAKE IT BETTER, MAKE IT SHORTER

Which speech do you remember: Lincoln's Gettysburg Address, clocking in at just over two minutes and 268 words or Edward Everett's two-hour 13,607 word odyssey that preceded it?

If you're asking, "Who is Edward Everett?" then you have obviously answered the question.

We have a tendency to think that a long speech is a good speech, yet anytime we have to actually sit through a long speech, we suffer from the boredom and the agony of feeling forced to sit through an extended speech that says much without saying anything at all.

We've got to do something about that.

Everyone's Got Something to Add... Unfortunately

I was in a working meeting wherein a colleague asked for feedback on an upcoming presentation she was to give. She spoke for about 20 minutes, and then asked us to provide feedback on how to improve the presentation. Everyone had something to say, but it mostly revolved around making it longer. They suggested adding more technical language, explaining in greater detail broader concepts, more slides with more data, and on and on.

We've got to do something about that.

The Simple Solution—What You Can Do

You want to make it better? Make it shorter.

If you have twenty slides, make it nineteen. If you have nineteen slides, cut it to eighteen.

If you have 13,000 words, cut to 10,000. If you can, cut down to 500. Your audience will be grateful. No one appreciates a speech or presentation that is long for the sake of being long.

Take a topic, determine what needs to be said to get the job done effectively, and be done with it. Of course, don't cut out the meaning or the understanding. However, there's no need to add words for its own sake.

WHAT MORE CAN I SAY?

A colleague of mine once said about working on a paper (or in this case, a book) that you never really finish it; you simply have to stop at some point. I think this is especially true in this case.

I'm sure that as soon as I send this off to the publisher, I'll think of ten or fifteen other things I want to add. Of course, if I did that, the book would grow and grow until even Proust would say, "Enough!"

Actually, additional thoughts and techniques can be found on the website (www.prettygoodspeech.com) where I invite you to check periodically for updates and to provide feedback. Need some question answered that wasn't included in the book? Let me know, and I'll address it!

I sincerely hope that this book proves useful to you. As I've been saying all along, the only way to improve as a speaker or a speech writer is to continue doing it. It's not easy and it's not always fun. Most of the time, you don't even notice any progress. But with the guidance of a pretty good speech instructor (named Mark… Woods… you know, the guy who wrote this book), and lot of work and practice, you'll be more than just a pretty good speaker. You'll be an even better speaker.

There's no limit to what you can accomplish if you just believe that it's possible and work hard to make it happen. Good public speaking can be an end unto itself, but I know that you will find that it will open doors to many other things, and that the dreams you have and the goals you set will be more easily realized with the skills you develop here and now.

I wish you all the best.

Speak up. Speak often. Speak well.

APPENDIX

INTERVIEWS: APPLYING PUBLIC SPEAKING SKILLS

One of the questions you may ask about public speaking is, "Other than giving a speech, what's the use of having these skills?" This implies that these skills do not translate into other areas of your life, and therefore are useless. However, a better way to ask that questions is, "How can my public speaking skills help me in other areas of my life?"

How about your next job interview?

That's right; the job interview requires many of the same skills used to deliver a speech. Unfortunately, we have a tendency to compartmentalize our skills rather than to see wider applications. We think that public speaking is public speaking and interviews are interviews– apples and oranges. But if you take the same approach to your interview, you'll find that the process is much less daunting and the prospects of success are enhanced.

So, here are a few items to consider for your next interview.

Think of interview questions as a persuasive speech

Ultimately, you are trying to persuade the interviewer that you are the best candidate (for the job or the grant or whatever). You want to go from not having the job to having the job. That sounds like change, which is persuasion (see "Persuasion: Assessing the Need for Change"). When you think of each question as a persuasive speech or each answer you give as a persuasive argument (i.e. a main point), you'll begin to see the interview as a process of change. Every word, then, should be chosen to help the interviewer to see why choosing you is the best possible option.

Have prepared answers for tough interview questions.

When you know you are going to speak to an audience, you typically like to prepare the speech. Very few people enjoy the impromptu speech, which is what the interview typically feels like. But, does it have to be?

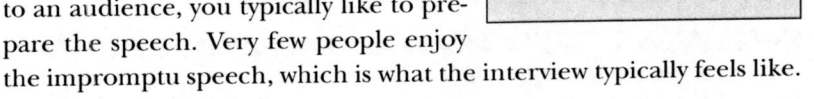

Honestly, no, it doesn't. You've been to an interview or two before, or at least you've read enough about them to know some of the tougher questions asked. While I can't provide an exhaustive list, some of the more common ones include:

- tell me about yourself (not actually a question, but…)
- where do you see yourself in five years? Ten years?
- what is your greatest strength/weakness?
- what do you know about us?
- Why should I hire you?

You know these questions are coming, and yet you don't have a fully-prepared answer for them. So, instead, your eyes go wide, you fumble for the words for a minute, and you look like you are scrambling to come up with something.

Or, you can sit down, think about the question, and think about what arguments you can provide that will help the interviewer see that you really are the best qualified candidate.

There's no shame in having a full response ready (even memorized) for the interviewer. Knowing what you plan to say will give you a boost of confidence when answering those tough questions.

By the way, they're all tough questions when you don't have a good answer.

Show you know the company (do your research)

Similar to having prepared answers about yourself, be sure to know the company inside and out. Who are the major decision-makers? How does your prospective job fit into the organization? What does the company value? How is the company doing? Who is their competition? And on and on....

Then, as you build your persuasive arguments, add in that knowledge. It provides support to your ultimate argument of being the best qualified candidate. Why? Because the best candidates do their homework and know their stuff.

Moreover, the more you know about them, the more you'll know if you are a good fit for the company. Don't just come in knowing that they'll pay more than your last job. Determine if the work will be fulfilling or if the working environment will suit you. There's no point going to an interview for a company you know will make you miserable.

Provide adequate eye contact

Again, it seems so obvious. Eye contact implies a connection between individuals communicating. People appreciate this connection. If you need proof, try to hold a conversation with a friend without eye contact. See how long it takes before he asks you if anything is the matter.

Remember that the interviewer is a person, and that person is probably as uncomfortable asking these questions as you are answering them. Providing that connection through eye contact will help to ease that discomfort. Of course, that being said, be sure not to stare unceasingly. There is such a thing as too much eye contact.

Be lively

Eye contact becomes especially uncomfortable if the person staring has no personality. So, it is especially important to follow eye contact with a sense of liveliness. I've mentioned the need to have a lively face and lively voice, but it bears repeating in this case. Smile some, nod your head a bit while listening, stress important words, and otherwise be engaged in what is essentially a semi-scripted conversation/presentation. This liveliness will go a long way in helping the interviewer see that you are more than just a resume among many other resumes.

I wish it were as simple as that. There are plenty of other factors that need consideration, many of which are out of your control. You can be fully-prepared, do all your homework, say all the right things, look them in the eye, and show tremendous personality and still not get the job. It's a tough market out there, and there are a lot of qualified candidates all doing their homework and knocking the interviewers' socks off with a great presentation. But, that's not a reason to avoid these tips. In fact, knowing others are doing everything to gain a competitive advantage, it's all the more reason you need to apply these skills. As you improve, you will begin to see the opportunities open up for you.

FOR STUDENTS: THE SECRET TO SUCCESS (IN SCHOOL)

You're not in high school anymore, and if you are in high school, it's time to stop acting like it. As you sit in your classroom, look at how many other students are there: probably anywhere from 20-200. Let's say there are 95% of them will become employed in the near future, so 19 out of 20 or 190 out of 200. So, 20 of you are competing for 19 jobs. Of those jobs, how many of them will pay $100,000 or more? Probably just one, if that. Do you want that one? I assume that you do, otherwise, why are you in school?

So, we've established that you want the top job, and that 19 other people or 199 other people will also want that job, too. That's one class room. How big is your school? How many colleges are in your area? How many are in the country? Thousands are all gunning for the top jobs in our economy. What makes you so special that you think you deserve it over anyone else?

I admit that a lot of factors are involved, but if all things were equal, what one thing would determine your success? My guess is the quality of your communication resulting from the quality of your education. Only the best get the best. The rest get the rest.

So, what are you doing to maximize your potential? Are you a good student? I don't mean simply getting good grades. Enough begging and pleading and working the system can keep you on the Dean's List. That's no indication of the quality of your education. What do you remember? What do you apply? How do you handle problems? How do you solve or resolve them?

Perhaps it's time for you to start to take your education more seriously. However, the question is, how do you do that? Read more? Stay awake at night fretting over your homework? Look serious all the time? Of course not. There are some very simple ways to succeed in school (and life), and if you apply these five simple principles, you will find that your grades will improve (legitimately), you will retain more information, apply that information more usefully, and enjoy your education more fully.

- Rule 1: Be Accountable—No Excuses
- Rule 2: Plan Ahead
- Rule 3: Take Notes
- Rule 4: Ask Questions
- Rule 5: Find Utility

Be Accountable—No Excuses

It's so funny how we spend so much time developing reasons to explain our actions rather than to simply change our actions. I have a friend who told me she wanted to come watch my hockey game, but did not show up. When I saw her she said, "I was really tired, and I didn't feel great, so I went to bed early. But I wanted to be there."

Of course, in the nicest way possible, I told her this simple truth: "If you really wanted to be there, then you would have been there."

The truth is, she really wanted to be asleep, and so she ultimately did what she wanted. And, that's okay, as long as you are honest about it. That's what accountability is all about.

Now, this isn't about me feeling disappointed that someone didn't show up to watch beer league hockey. It's about being accountable as a student. So, when you don't get an assignment completed or you don't show up for class, you have to accept responsibility for that. Ultimately, you chose not to complete the assignment or not to come to class.

The problem with excuses is that, even if they are true and legitimate, they still sound like excuses. I've had students tell me that it was too hot outside to go to class. I appreciate the honesty, at the very least. I've had students tell me that a relative has died or that they had a boyfriend who got in a car accident and she spent all night in the emergency ward. Again, it might all be true, but ultimately, we made choices not to do the work or show up.

Would you find a way to get to class or complete the assignment if there was $10 million waiting for you there to pick up? Suddenly it's not that hot outside, is it? Some people might say that this is horrible to say, but would you leave your grieving family or ailing boyfriend to pick up a $10 million check? If so, then not completing the assignment or attending class seem less excusable.

As a student, you are an adult free to make choices. But, as an adult, you must accept the consequences of your actions. If you know smoking is bad for you, but you choose to do it, then you can't be upset when you develop complications due to smoking. If you choose not to come to class, then you are accepting that you may not learn something covered in that time. If you don't turn in an assignment, you must be willing to accept a zero on that assignment. These are the consequences of your choices.

Once you do that, instructors will certainly have a great deal more respect for you. It does not take much for you to hold yourself accountable, yet it seems to be a rare quality. But, it is that very person who accepts consequences of their actions that often is given more leeway. How is that done?

Plan Ahead

The answer is far simpler than you think: plan ahead. If you know you can't make it to class, tell your instructors in advance, the further out, the better. Telling your professor two weeks in advance that you won't be able to attend class says a lot about how you feel about your education. It implies that you care enough to approach the instructor with a problem that will affect your ability to maximize your education, and that you are seeking a solution. You may find that they will allow you to turn in an assignment early or late. They might provide you with lecture notes or help you make arrangements to get notes from a student. Of course, the instructors will not always give you a break, but that's not what this is about. Knowing that you will be absent, you can now make the choice to complete assignments early or seek notes in time. Planning ahead gives you that opportunity. After all, there are many reasons, but there are no excuses.

Take Notes

What's the point of coming to class? Ideally, it's to learn. But, in a typical lecture, a lot of information is handled. It's very difficult to remember everything that was mentioned or discussed. That's where good notes come in.

Notes serve as a reminder of material discussed. They help you remember things said in class. But, they are so much more than that. Notes also serve as a guide to reading through your text books. The ideas presented in your notes (should) reflect what was covered in the readings, and will help you focus on what's important (in the mind of the instructor).

Ask Questions

Another important skill in maximizing your education is asking questions to help clarify ideas. When you aren't sure about an idea presented, ask questions. It's important for you to understand. If you don't understand, then you will find the next idea more difficult to grasp, as some ideas are built upon one another.

A side effect of asking questions is that the instructors know you are engaged in the discussion and that you want to learn. Remember, they are human, too, and it feels good to feel like you are helping someone, especially when helping someone learn.

Find Utility

The worst feeling about being in class is that sense that the stuff you are learning is completely useless. If it's useless, it will be very difficult to remember. It will also be very difficult to understand. Part of the reason is that you don't care because you think it has no use for you.

However, anything you learn can be useful to some degree at some point. The trick is to ask how it can be used in the future. Students often don't think that they will do much public speaking in the future, so they fail to see how acquiring these communication skills will serve them in the future. But, if you find that you are in a job interview or giving a presentation or simply trying to convince a customer to purchase a product, the skills of public speaking become extremely valuable.

So, for everything you learn, every subject, every fact, think of ways that the information can be of use to you in the future. It might be obscure, but you never know. It may be some little fact that you bring up at a dinner party that might impress someone who happens to be looking for a few intelligent people to help run her new Fortune 500 company, and she wants you to call her for an interview. You never know!

The Key to Being a Good Student

Being a good student isn't a trick to help you scam your way into an extra few days to turn in an assignment or get an excused absence or a boosted grade. It's really about being good to yourself and taking care of your future. It's about taking the long view. Memorizing notes for an exam is a time-honored tradition, but so is forgetting 90% of it as soon as the test is over. Taking a moment to think through the ideas presented to you in class and in texts will help you remember what you've learned and help you to find a way to use that information to be as successful as you want to be. Ultimately, that's what it's all about: success.